FLYING

TO

GLORY

Plays by Sandra Dempsey

Full Length Plays
D'Arcy
Enigma
Wings of the Albatross

Comedies (with music)
Blue Collar Blues
The Cuff 'n' Billy Show
That's No Lady, That's My Immigrant

One Act Plays
Armagideon
Eight To Four
Requiem

Short Plays
Barbie & Ken
Barbie und Ken
Casualties
Clap-Trap
Legacy
Officer Drag
Orders
Pee-pipe
Pierre Là
Rosa's Lament
Wings and A Prayer

Flying

to

Glory

Prairie boys take flight in the
Royal Canadian Air Force
in World War II

a drama
by

Sandra Dempsey

Touchwood Press

sd@SandraDempsey.com, www.SandraDempsey.com

Sandra Dempsey, c/o Playwrights Guild of Canada
2nd floor, 54 Wolseley Street, Toronto, ON M5T 1A5
Phone 416-703-0201, www.PlaywrightsGuild.ca

Sandra Dempsey, c/o The Writers' Union of Canada
200 - 90 Richmond Street East, Toronto, ON M5C 1P1
Phone 416-703-8982, www.writersunion.ca

Library and Archives Canada Cataloguing in Publication

Dempsey, Sandra
    Flying to glory : Prairie boys take flight in the Royal Canadian Air Force in World War II : a drama / by Sandra Dempsey.

A play.
ISBN 0-9687861-6-2

    1. Canada. Royal Canadian Air Force–Drama. 2. British Commonwealth Air Training Plan–Drama. 3. World War, 1939-1945–Aerial operations, Canadian–Drama. 4. World War, 1939-1945–Canada–Drama. I. Title.

PS8557.E4825F59 2006   C812'.54   C2006-902874-5

Touchwood Press
6228 Touchwood Drive NW
Calgary AB T2K 3L9
E-mail: jlfrey@telusnet.com

Printed and bound in Canada by Priority Printing, Edmonton, Alberta
Book Design and Production: John Frey
Cover Illustration: Permission to reproduce Michael McCabe's painting "Invincible Item" was provided by courtesy of the artist and Halifax 57 Rescue (Canada).

for those who served, those who flew,
those who touched shed angels' wings

As a living legacy, the playwright suggests that a percentage
of box office revenues from performances and productions of
Flying To Glory will be donated by producers to the Royal
Canadian Air Force Benevolent Fund, the Royal Canadian
Legion, or a similar WWII veterans' charity, or the Halifax 57
Rescue (Canada) recovery project.

CONTENTS

THE PLAY

APPENDICES

TIME

WWII, early 1942 to mid 1943

PLACE

City of Calgary and area, Training Bases in Calgary and Edmonton, Air Bases and Hospital in England, Aboard a Halifax bomber

CHARACTERS

Minimum: two females and eight males
Maximum: unlimited. The use of real air cadets and/or air force personnel as extras such as parade marching drills and/or ground crew is encouraged.

Main Characters
Jimmy (James) "Balzac" Edgerton Grady (Pilot Officer), age 18
Gus (Angus) "Rusky" Lyle Minton (Flying Officer), age 19
Shirley Grady, age 46
Betty (Elizabeth) Lipton, age 20
Hillis, Harold (Harry) K. "Hops" Hillis (R.A.A.F. Flight Sergeant), age 18

Secondary Characters (doubling permitted and encouraged)
Graziano Angelo Marchitelli (pronounced *grats-ee-ano mark-i-telly,* Italian-Canadian Flight Lieutenant Grant March), age 21
R.A.F. Flight Sgnt. (U.K. Flight Engineer) Fred "Skinner" Langdon, age 19
R.C.A.F. Flight Sgnt. (Wireless Operator) Francis "Fever" Felverton, age 20
R.A.F. Flight Sgnt. (U.K. Mid Upper Gunner) Quinton Darby, age 24
R.C.A.F. Flight Sgnt. (Tail Gunner) Louis "Frenchy" Brébuf, age 18
R.C.A.F. Recruitment Sergeant, age 36
Rejected Recruit, age 39
Civilian Flying Instructor Chalmers, E.F.T.S. No.5 High River, age 23
Civilian Flying Instructor Reid, E.F.T.S. No.5 High River, age 29
Chief Flying Instructor (C.F.I.), E.F.T.S. No.5 High River, age 40
R.C.A.F. Commanding Officer (C.O.), E.F.T.S. No.5 High River, age 42
R.C.A.F. Flying Instructor, age 28

Secondary Characters Continued
A.C.2/LAC Charles "Chipper" Breverton, age 19
Group Captain, S.F.T.S. No.3, No.4 Training Command, Calgary, age 52
R.C.A.F. Health Instructor, age 47
R.C.A.F. Psychology Officer, age 49
Grace, age 43
Calgary Policeman/Saboteur, age 49
Corporal, No.3 Manning Depot/No.5 E.F.T.S., age 32
Pilot White, age 19
Pilot Black, age 21
Veteran R.A.F. Flight Engineer, age 25
R.A.F. Woodbridge Briefing Officer, age 46
R.C.A.F. Pilot Officer Liam Hannigan, age 22
Recruits, AC2s, LACs, Erks

Voices
R.C.A.F. Aircraft (A/C) Recognition Instructor
R.C.A.F. Wings Parade Corporal
R.C.A.F. Bournemouth Drill Sergeant
R.A.F. Pickersgill Commanding Officer (Commander)
R.A.F. Pickersgill Meteorology Officer (Met Man)
Commanding Officers

PROLOGUE

Betty, dressed in her R.C.A.F. Women's Division (W.D.) uniform, marches in from the left, comes to attention at centre stage. Facing the audience, she salutes, then stands at ease.

BETTY: Canada has gone to war right off the bat: September 1, 1939. Within one year, Canadian and British leaders decided that Canada should become the base for all Allied Commonwealth air training, and the British Commonwealth Air Training Plan was born. Volunteer aircrew trainees from Australia, New Zealand, and Britain will all travel to Canada to join Canadian volunteer trainees and learn to fly or crew Allied aircraft. Eventually, they will be joined by Norwegians, Free French, Belgians, Poles, South Africans, Rhodesians and Czechoslovakians. Canada will train over one hundred and thirty-one thousand aircrew. Of those, some fifty-five percent will be Canadians, seventy-two thousand, eight hundred and thirty-five to be exact. Seventy-two thousand post-pubescent Canadian boys, running amok all over the country!

They will train at three hundred and sixty air training schools across the country, eighteen of them in the province of Alberta. There will be seven hundred hangars and thousands of buildings, messes, canteens, drill halls, class rooms, and barracks. The majority of these flying schools will be on the wide open Canadian prairies. And soon everyone, from airman to civilian, will become all too familiar with the smells of this new air war: sweat on wool, heavy aviation oil, musky aircraft canvas, and ammunition cordite.

(beat) More than nine hundred recruits will die in training accidents and some ten thousand aircraft will be lost in training. But at its peak, Canada's R.C.A.F. will comprise the third largest air force in the world.

(frustrated) The poster says, "We Serve, So That Men May Fly." "There's A Place For You in the R.C.A.F. Women's Division." "But

you've got to get in on the ground floor," Pop said. "You can fly circles around those boys. They can't help but notice your flying hours," he said. So I joined. First, they only wanted W.D.s to cook and sew and answer telephones. Then, they got us packing silks, driving trucks. Now I fuel up the Annies and Harvards, and Sal's helping me with the mechanics so's I can work on the engines. *(giggles)* Me, mechanically inclined. I could go for a mechanic right now, alright.

They've got to need us to fly soon – they've just got to. And boy, when they do, I'm going to be the first in line.

Oh, uh, Sal – they call him Sal because his name's Sallows. All the boys have nicknames. Let's see, there's Dusty, Mac, Scotch, Chuck, Tommie, Spike, Chipper. Jimmy will probably get some crazy kind of nickname I won't ever understand. Same with Gus, too.

I'd give anything to be up there with them. The boys say they've already got my name all figured out. They say they're going to call me Ida – because Ida loaded my pants. Ida lost my lunch. Ida puked into my Gosport. Ida puked into my chute.

Ida beared-down and learned to loop-the-loop, but Ida greyed-out going up, and redded-out coming down. Ida got dizzy just from breathing so hard.

And every time Ida landed, Ida done a pranger. Ida run so many props into the runway and bent them backwards, Ida thought I could fly in reverse. Ida been paired up for cross-country with LAC Prune. And Ida tried to fly my kite due north to Edmonton, but Ida ended up going straight south to Montana.

But Ida got my air force wings. Ida done just what they asked. Up there it doesn't matter if you're a miss or a mister – you all die the same. *(pause)* And maybe Ida had my kite shot out from under me just like any of the boys. And I guess Ida ended up just as dead as any of them will, too.

> *A military band begins a spirited rendition of a tune such as the "Air Force March." Betty comes to attention and turns right. As she marches past, the lights come up on the Recruiting Depot down right and the scene comes to life.*

ACT ONE

SCENE 1

Recruitment Depot, outside the downtown Hudson's Bay store in Calgary. A Recruitment Sergeant enters and seats himself at a makeshift desk, before a long line of young civilian men waiting to volunteer. Jimmy, Gus and Graziano are just behind the first person.

RECRUITMENT SERGEANT: Alright! The air force is officially open for business, boys. Let's get all of you volunteers signed up and sent on your way, like the posters say, to Adventure in the Skies! Next!

An older man is first. He steps forward and offers his papers.

That's very good of you, sir, but what is your age?

MAN: *(very quietly)* Thirty-nine.

RECRUITMENT SERGEANT: *(loud)* Thirty-nine? Sorry, sir, but this is a young man's game. Take my word, you'd be as weak as fairy piss trying to keep control of an aeroplane under attack. Next!

The man reluctantly leaves.

JIMMY: Here, sir.

RECRUITMENT SERGEANT: *(scanning the papers)* "Grady" – not *the* Edgerton Grady?

JIMMY: Yes, sir, that was my father, Edgerton Grady. He flew for the Royal Flying Corps.

RECRUITMENT SERGEANT: Don't I know it. He was practically a legend with rudder and stick. Is he serving now?

JIMMY: Oh, no, sir. He never flew again after the Huns tore up his Camel.

RECRUITMENT SERGEANT: Oh, I remember my old man used to tell me he got jumped by the Red Baron! And he got his lungs burned bad from the fire, didn't he?

JIMMY: *(a little embarrassed)* Well, it wasn't exactly the Red Baron but something like that. The crash was pretty bad, and he's been at the veterans hospital since he got back.

RECRUITMENT SERGEANT: Too bad. Well, kid, you'll do him proud.

JIMMY: Yes, sir.

RECRUITMENT SERGEANT: Sign here.

> *Jimmy signs.*

That's it, lad. *(standing)* And I'm going to give you your first flying lesson right here and now. The R.C.A.F. salute: *(demonstrating)* roundhouse up, palm facing forward, like you're showing you don't have anything in your hand, straight down. Do it with me: roundhouse up, palm facing forward, straight down. And you're in the air force.

> *Jimmy simultaneously salutes.*

Now, take these papers, fill out these forms, and go straight through there.

> *Jimmy takes the paperwork but hesitates.*

Oh, alright. You can wait for your chums here – only in deference to your Dad. But don't get your hopes up. Odds are the three of you won't stay together much past enlisting, you know.

JIMMY: No, sir. Thank you, sir. *(he salutes and steps aside to wait)*

Gus moves to the front of the line.

RECRUITMENT SERGEANT: *(he notes his jeans and chuckles)* You won't be seeing your Cowboy Kings for a long time. Name?

GUS: Angus Lyle Minton. *(he hands over his paperwork)*

RECRUITMENT SERGEANT: *(glancing through the papers)* Excellent marks. Ever been up in an aeroplane?

GUS: No, sir. But I'm a quick learner, and keen.

RECRUITMENT SERGEANT: Let's hope so. Sign here, take this, fill in these.

> *Gus takes the paperwork and joins Jimmy.*

And last but not least...

> *Graziano moves up and hands over his paperwork. The sergeant's pencil breaks.*

Damn. Just a minute, son. *(sharpening his pencil)* How 'bout you? Ever been near an aeroplane?

GRAZIANO: Yes, sir. I'm actually one lesson short of getting my pilot's license, sir. And my instructor has written a letter regarding my current level of skill.

> *Graziano offers the letter and the Recruitment Sergeant glances at the letterhead.*

RECRUITMENT SERGEANT: *(reading the letterhead)* Calgary Flying Club, now we're talking. *(he goes back to filling out the first form)* Okay, son, and your name is?

GRAZIANO: Graziano Angelo Marchitelli.

RECRUITMENT SERGEANT: Grats... *(stops dead and looks up)* What did you say?

GRAZIANO: Graziano Angelo Marchitelli.

RECRUITMENT SERGEANT: You've got to be kidding, right?

GRAZIANO: *(confused)* No, sir.

RECRUITMENT SERGEANT: You've got some nerve, showing up here of all places. Now take your stinking papers and get the hell out of my sight! *(throwing the papers at Graziano)*

GRAZIANO: Sir? I don't understand...

RECRUITMENT SERGEANT: *(standing up)* What's to understand! Now pick up your goddamned papers and whatever else you've got and get the hell out of here, you goddamned wop!

GUS: What the hell?

GRAZIANO: What did you call me?

RECRUITMENT SERGEANT: *(shouting)* Get the hell out of here, you stinking dago!

JIMMY: Sir, he's our friend...

GUS: Back off, sir!

RECRUITMENT SERGEANT: *(to Gus and Jimmy)* No boy, you back off. One step closer and you're both out of the air force! Now stay out of this! *(to Graziano)* As for you, the only so-called wop in this air force is the famous bush pilot Wop May who's a Commanding Officer now – and he got that name 'cause it's the sound of a propeller, not because he's got enemy blood in his veins! Now if you don't get the hell out of here, I'll have you arrested!

GRAZIANO: I don't understand. I'm perfectly suitable to join the air force.

RECRUITMENT SERGEANT: Canada is at war with Italy!

GRAZIANO: But I'm Canadian! I was born right here in Alberta!

RECRUITMENT SERGEANT: I don't care if you were born out of the sap from a maple tree! No goddamned grape-stomper is going to get into the Royal Canadian Air Force through my recruitment station!

Gus and Jimmy hold Graziano back from coming to blows with the Recruitment Sergeant.

GRAZIANO: Let me at him!

GUS: He's volunteering and you're refusing him?

RECRUITMENT SERGEANT: *(to Gus and Jimmy)* If you two don't back off now, you'll be out of the air force before you even get in!

GRAZIANO: I've practically got my pilot's license, I'm volunteering to fly and fight for my country, and you won't let me join because my family is Italian?

RECRUITMENT SERGEANT: "Your country?" See, that's exactly the problem, because ten-to-one you'd be fighting for the wrong side.

Betty comes running in.

BETTY: *(calling out)* Grats! Grats! Oh, I'm so glad I caught you before you signed up. *(she sees the Recruitment Sergeant, comes to attention and salutes)* Beg your pardon, sir. But I have an urgent message for the recruit.

RECRUITMENT SERGEANT: *(he returns the salute while still face to face with Graziano)* I only see two recruits. If you have a message for this... gentleman, then give it to him on his way out.

BETTY: Thank you, sir. *(pulling Graziano aside)* Grats, what's going on here?

GRAZIANO: *(eyeing the Recruitment Sergeant)* That's a good question.

BETTY: Grats, you've got to get home! Right now!

GRAZIANO: What?

BETTY: Mounties came to your house – they're trying to take your Papa away to an internment camp! For the duration of the war!

GRAZIANO: What? No, no. That's the Japs. It's the Japs in Vancouver. They're shipping them all to internment camps in British Columbia. Not the Italians.

BETTY: No, I swear, Grats, now they're doing it to the Italians, here, too. The one mountie told me it's been happening since way before Pearl Harbour, but there's Italian families all across the country so it's been taking a lot longer. Apparently, there's a camp in Kananaskis. He said they're finally checking the names in Alberta, and Calgary, and that means your family! Grats, they're trying to take your Papa!

GRAZIANO: *(horrified)* He's an old man, for god's sake! And he's a Canadian citizen now! They can't do that!

BETTY: That doesn't seem to matter. *(pulling Graziano further aside and lowering her voice)* Look, you've got to get home to your Mamma. She's just beside herself, she's so upset. She needs you. Whether or not you can get the R.C.M.P. to let your Papa stay, you'll have to figure that out later. Right now, you've just got to get home, okay? Come on, *(whispering)* I have an officer's car, I can drive you, but we have to go right now.

GRAZIANO: *(reluctant)* Alright. *(shaking the hands of Jimmy and Gus)* Good-bye. Good luck. We made a pact to get this far. We'll meet up again. Somewhere, somehow.

JIMMY: *(quietly)* Good luck to you, Grats.

Graziano and Betty run off.

RECRUITMENT SERGEANT: *(he dusts off his clothes and regains his composure)* How do you like that? Problem solved. *(pause)* Now, you two. You've got one decision to make. You can either walk through there, straight into the air force, or you can tail after your friend there, and you'll never get anywhere near the R.C.A.F. ever again.

Jimmy and Gus are torn. Finally, Gus moves back to processing and Jimmy follows.

Good lads. That's the stuff. You won't regret it. *(calling to the line)* Next!

The lights fade out on the Recruitment Depot.

SCENE 2

No.3 Manning Depot, Edmonton. Jimmy and Gus and a group of new R.C.A.F. recruits enter sweeping with large push brooms. They are all dressed in baggy cotton sweatpants, sweatshirts and side caps.

GUS: Fly in the frigging sky! All we've done so far is march and sweep cow patties and march and sweep cow patties. And when we were finished with that, what do you know, we did something new! We marched and swept road apples! The pride of Alberta, Canada's best budding flyboys, "Men With A Purpose" sweeping up Royal Canadian Air Force cow patties and road apples!

JIMMY: Well, it's an exhibition grounds. I guess we should have expected it. There's no silver plate and room service in this place.

GUS: I expect to be high in the frigging sky, not doubled over with my nose to the floor, rearranging manure.

They both lean on their brooms for a break.

CORPORAL: *(shouts from off-stage)* Quit standing around or you'll get a broom up your hinny backsides!

The recruits all resume sweeping strenuously.

Company, Fall In!

The recruits drop their brooms and form a line abreast. The Corporal strides in, behind the line, holding a clipboard.

Not that way, this way! About face!

The recruits pivot awkwardly to face upstage.

Air Craftsmen 2nd Class, that's what you are, second class citizens, lowest of the low. And you think you're good enough to join the Royal Canadian Air Force? *(shakes his head)* What a mangy bunch of knuckleheads. You're so useless you wouldn't amount to a row of pins. God help Initial Training School, if you make it that far. *(shouts)* Alright now, hang out!

The recruits don't know what to do.

(shouts) I said hang out!

The recruits are still confused.

I don't believe this! It's a short-arm inspection! Now unzip and hang out!

The recruits awkwardly and shyly comply.

(making his way along the line, inspecting their genitals and charting his comments and grumbling as he goes) Saddest looking bunch of... it's going to take a hell of a long war to get you jerks into the sky. I don't know if the Nazis can wait that long! Alright, close it up!

The recruits fumble to re-zip. Everybody's side cap pops shut in the process.

RECRUIT 1: *(caught in his zipper)* Ow!

Gus laughs out loud and Jimmy can't help but join in. The Corporal glares and they stop.

CORPORAL: *(shouts)* About face!

The line pivots awkwardly to face downstage.

Is there anyone who has not been given his uniform? *(no response)* Good. Is there anyone who thinks he has the wrong size of uniform?

All recruits raise their hands.

Tough. Find yourself a civilian tailor and get your uniform fitting perfectly. If you wear the R.C.A.F. uniform, you must look impeccable. We'll worry about substance later.

GUS: *(half-raises his hand)* Uh, sir?

The Corporal glares at him.

Uh, I have a problem with my side cap. It keeps popping shut.

CORPORAL: I don't care if you have to duct tape it to your head, but when you are in uniform, you are expected to keep your side cap on your frigging heads. If you can't accomplish that little task, then I suggest you go home and listen to the war on your mommy's radio.

GUS: Yes, sir.

CORPORAL: Now, we're going to begin the first of what will be many medical testing sessions to determine whether or not you are air force material. These M-2s have all been scientifically designed, and the results of your progress in these tests will be overseen by the Medical Officer. And believe you me, there are no short cuts. *(demonstrating as he goes)* Now, on my command, you will stand on your right leg, left leg bent back at the knee, arms outstretched like this, and eyes closed. Everyone, let me see you do that.

The recruits try to comply.

I said stand on your right leg, recruit, not your left. Now, remaining in this position, everyone begin hopping up and down.

The recruits begin hopping, all a wriggling line of lost balance, forgetting to stretch out arms, using the wrong leg, etc.

Minerva, it's going to be one long war... *(shouts)* Alright, halt. Attention!

Again, with many errors and bad timing, the recruits eventually come to attention.

If you want to make it into the training program and get anywhere near flying in the sky, I suggest that every waking hour, you practice this exercise. Now, double-time, on the spot, go!

The recruits jog in place.

Up, up, up, up! Knees and arms, up, Mother Brown! And stop. *(he blows his whistle)*

I see running is a foreign subject to most of you, so you can count on lots of practice in that skill, too. For now, I want you to clean up this barn until it's so spic and span you can eat off the floor. Get sweeping!

The recruits sweep enthusiastically.

I can't guarantee that you won't have to eat off the floor, so you'd better do a good job. I want you to pick up every single strand of straw, every little thing on the floor. If it doesn't move, paint it; if you can't paint it, salute it; if you can't salute it, go join the frigging navy! Now carry on!

The Corporal exits and the recruits return to their sweeping.

GUS: Hopping? I'm going to learn to fly by hopping?

JIMMY: Beats me. Let's hope it's just a balance thing.

Music, such as "The Maple Leaf Forever", is heard in the distance.

GUS: Hey, what's that?

JIMMY: I'm guessing it's the Wings Parade for the class before us.

GUS: Wings Parade. Well, it looks like the only thing we'll be getting is a brooms parade. I mean it. If this keeps up they won't need to teach me running because I'll be running right out of here.

Two pilots enter. They have just graduated.

PILOT WHITE: *(shouts)* Attention! Form up!

The recruits come to attention with their brooms at their sides, facing downstage.

PILOT BLACK: What's the matter with you men? Officer White, why aren't these men in position?

PILOT WHITE: It's inexcusable, sir. *(shouts)* Recruits, drop them!

The recruits hesitate.

JIMMY: Begging your pardon, sir, but we just had a short-arm inspection.

PILOT BLACK: I don't care what you just did, recruit! This is an inoculation. You haven't been inoculated yet, have you?

JIMMY: No sir.

PILOT BLACK: No you haven't! Just for that insolence, recruit, you can donate five dollars to...

PILOT WHITE: *(thinking fast)*...to Air Vice Marshal Prune's recovery fund and cleaning bill. He crashed landed into the latrines.

PILOT BLACK: *(stifling his laughter)* Right! Now hand it over.

JIMMY: *(hurrying to find his money in his sock)* I'm afraid I only have a ten, sir.

PILOT BLACK: Oh, well, we'll see that you get your change back.

JIMMY: Thank you sir.

PILOT WHITE: Now, drop your drawers and bend over!

The recruits drop their sweatpants, leaving their undershorts up.

(shouts) Shorts, too, you idiots!

The recruits pull the backs of their shorts down to reveal their upper buttocks and bend over from the waist.

Now, Officer Black, you may proceed with your orders.

PILOT BLACK: Yes, sir. *(to the recruits)* You heard the officer. Now don't move so much as an inch!

Pilot White and Pilot Black stifle their laughter and exit waving the money. The Corporal returns, to the sight of all the recruits bent over showing their upper buttocks.

CORPORAL: Now what the hell is going on here? *(shouts)* Pull up your pants! *(to Jimmy)* You, what the hell are you doing sticking your posterior in my face?

JIMMY: We were awaiting our inoculation, sir.

CORPORAL: What? What inoculation?

JIMMY: Don't know, sir. Officer Black didn't specify, sir.

CORPORAL: Officer Black? Who the hell is Officer Black?

GUS: *(pipes in)* I believe it was the same Officer Black who took up the collection for the Air Vice Marshal, sir.

CORPORAL: Air Vice Marshal?

GUS: *(completely serious)* Yes, sir. Air Vice Marshal Prune. You know, after he crashed-landed into the latrines.

CORPORAL: *(sarcastic)* Oh! Air Vice Marshal Prune! *(shouts)* Well the Vice Marshal inoculates you with five laps double time around the parade square. Now form up and move!

The recruits hurry into march formation, shoulder their brooms and jog out.

SCENE 3

No.4 Initial Training School (I.T.S.) Edmonton. The sound of a column of airmen marching is heard. Recruits are now dressed in their R.C.A.F. uniforms and side caps. Two recruits enter together and pose for a picture as a camera flash illuminates them. They repeat the pose, in reverse, and another flash goes off. Gradually Jimmy and Gus enter, reading the front page of a newspaper. Other recruits enter and crowd around trying to read the story.

ALL RECRUITS: Hurray!

A/C INSTRUCTOR VOICE: Gentlemen, what is going on?

The recruits snap to attention.

CHIPPER: A Canadian pilot in a Kittyhawk shot down a Jap Zero off the Aleutians!

A/C INSTRUCTOR VOICE: Yes, it's terrific news alright. But let's get back to business.

Large black silhouettes of aircraft are projected, one by one, onto the faces of the class.

There's an aeroplane before you. What is it?

JIMMY: *(he raises his hand)* Junkers Fifty-two. *(he raises his hand)* De Havilland "Mossie" Mosquito.

GUS: *(he raises his hand)* Folke-Wulf one-ninety.

CHIPPER: *(he raises his hand)* Handley Page Hampden.

GUS: *(he raises his hand)* Westland Lizzie – I mean, Lysander.

JIMMY: *(he raises his hand)* Heinkel one-eleven. *(he raises his hand)* Short Sterling. *(he raises his hand)* Messerschmitt one-o-nine.

GUS: *(he raises his hand)* Bristol Blenheim. *(as the Spitfire appears, the entire class raise their hands)*

ALL: *(in unison)* Supermarine Spitfire.

JIMMY: *(he raises his hand)* Junkers eighty-seven, Stuka. *(he raises his hand)* Dornier two seventeen. *(he raises his hand)* Hawker Hurricane.

GUS: *(he raises his hand)* Handley Page Wellington.

JIMMY: *(he raises his hand)* Bristol Beaufighter. *(he raises his hand)* Bristol Bolingbroke. *(he raises his hand)* Lockheed Hudson.

GUS: *(whispers to Jimmy)* So long as all the enemy kites hold nice and still like that, we should be just fine.

Jimmy and Gus laugh.

A/C INSTRUCTOR VOICE: You two, stand up!

Jimmy and Gus jump up.

Names!

JIMMY: Air Craftsman 2nd Class James E. Grady, Sir.

GUS: Air Craftsman 2nd Class Angus L. Minton, Sir.

A/C INSTRUCTOR VOICE: Grady and Minton. Very kind of you two gentlemen to give up your next forty-eight to work guard duty. Sit.

The embarrassment of being singled out causes Gus to have the stirrings of an erection. Jimmy and Gus sink back into their chairs as the lights come up on Health Class. The Health Instructor enters in mid lecture, with a chart, easel and pointer.

Throughout, the airmen snicker at provocative words and diagrams, and Gus squirms in his seat, his erection growing.

HEALTH INSTRUCTOR: *(in mid sentence)...* you should all know about venereal disease. Of course, alcohol is dangerous, in that it may make you expose yourself to infection.

CHIPPER: *(loud whisper)* I was exposed but it didn't take!

HEALTH INSTRUCTOR: Believe you me, men, you don't want to take it home with you. V.D. is just as bad after the war as during the war. You want to return to your family and loved ones free from disease and in perfect health.

How do you do that, you may ask? By controlling your urges, that's how. Sexual impulses may be controlled by deviation into other channels of activity, such as football, ice hockey, carpentry. Wholesome companionship with members of the opposite sex is desirable, but be on your guard.

Personal protection is paramount – *(he proudly sets up a pun)* But when you do mount a pair... *(dead silence as nobody gets it)*...ahem – well – personal decontamination is foremost. Remember this word: RUSKS! R-U-S-K-S.

R for Rubber Condom, U for Urinate, S for Soap and water, and K for Kit or V-pak, and S for S.E.P.T., your Service Early Preventative Treatment station. If you remember nothing else, remember this. As the film says, "It's Up To You." Any questions? *(checking his watch)* Very well. Mess in five minutes. Class dismissed.

As the recruits stand to attention, gather up their belongings and leave, Gus lags behind and grabs a book to hide his erection.

GUS: Pssst!

JIMMY: *(he sees Gus and claps his hands in mock applause)* Ladies and Ladies! We present Alberta's own, winner of the I.T.S. Fastest Flyer Award! Let's give him a hand... well, no, I guess he doesn't really need another hand. Congratulations, "Rusky!" *(he laughs)*

GUS: Pipe down, wise guy! Just walk nonchalant ahead of me for a while.

JIMMY: Glad to – only you mean a real short while.

GUS: Just go!

> *They exit.*

SCENE 4

> *Jimmy checks that his uniform is perfect as he awaits his turn to see the R.C.A.F. Psychology Officer. Gus is just finishing his session.*

GUS: *(exiting the Psychology Officer's office, carrying a paper and talking over his shoulder)* ...but I never would!

PSYCHOLOGY OFFICER: *(shouting after Gus)* But if you ever did!

GUS: But I never would!

PSYCHOLOGY OFFICER: *(shouting)* Shut up, before I change my mind!

GUS: *(mimes zippering his mouth closed, then unzips and loudly whispers)* Never happen, sir! Never! *(to Jimmy)* Jimmsy, you'll have to stay on your toes for this one! That shrink's a regular nut case!

> *Gus punches Jimmy in the shoulder as they pass. Gus exits. Jimmy enters the Psychology Officer's office, comes to attention and salutes, then remains standing.*

PSYCHOLOGY OFFICER: *(without looking up)* Grady, is that right?

JIMMY: Yes, sir.

PSYCHOLOGY OFFICER: *(looking up)* I recognize the name.

JIMMY: Yes, sir. My father flew for the Royal Flying Corps.

PSYCHOLOGY OFFICER: Right. Well, that's a good bloodline, but it won't help you as far as I'm concerned.

JIMMY: No, sir.

PSYCHOLOGY OFFICER: You see, young man, the job of a Psychology Officer is to determine whether or not you're Royal Canadian Air Force material. It's an inexplicable sort of thing, but whatever it is, you must have it. Some believe it's heart or guts or some such. But it's all of those, and more. It must be a part of you, down to your very soul. It must be in your blood, if you know what I mean.

JIMMY: Yes, sir.

PSYCHOLOGY OFFICER: Well, why don't you tell me why it is you want to learn to fly aeroplanes.

JIMMY: Um, there's nothing I wouldn't do to learn to fly. I don't have any outstanding skills or anything, at least not yet. But I've wanted to fly ever since I was a kid. I remember, I was about nine years old or thereabouts, and I liked to take my Pop's old binoculars out onto the prairie and just watch the hawks and sometimes eagles soaring up there in the cloudless blue, looking to find a prairie squirrel or gopher or anything. And I remember one day I picked out this big, beautiful peregrine, just circling and circling high above – I know now he must have been riding the hot thermal air currents. Just circling and circling, completely quiet. Not flapping his wings, just soaring with his wings spread out full. They must have been six feet or more from wingtip to wingtip. Anyway, I just kept watching him, and the more I watched, the more I started to feel like I was flying.

PSYCHOLOGY OFFICER: Oh?

JIMMY: Oh, not that I was drunk or anything! No, no. In fact, if anything, I suppose I could have been hallucinating a little, just from being out in the hot sun for so long and not having any water with me. But I just kept watching that hawk, and he kept turning his head from side to side, looking for his prey. Round and round, he kept scanning the earth below, and checking in the air for competition or predators at the same time.

But all of a sudden, that beautiful, soaring peregrine hawk turned his head all the way to look *behind*. And right then and there, I thought, I want to do that. I want to be up there, flying in the air, keeping myself flying, and be able to look wherever I want, and even be able to look behind me and still keep on flying! I want to have complete control of my Spitfire and be able to hunt my prey, and keep from being hunted – and I know I can do it. If someone will just teach me to fly, and sit me in a Spitfire, I know I can do it. *(quiet, awkward)* I guess it sounds a little weird, but that's when I knew I wanted to grow up to learn to fly.

    Pause.

PSYCHOLOGY OFFICER: Son, if I had a nickel for every boy here who claims to have been inspired by some bird way off in the prairie sky... Tell me, if you had just left your house and you were to board a train on the hour, and you suddenly thought you'd left the oven on at your house, would you board your train on time or run back home first?

JIMMY: I'd board the train, sir.

PSYCHOLOGY OFFICER: You would? Even though your house might burn to the ground?

JIMMY: Yes, sir.

PSYCHOLOGY OFFICER: Well. Alright. What the heck. You kept such a straight face during your story, so who am I not to humour you.

    He puts his signature to a form and hands it to Jimmy.

Take this to the office and they'll assign you to a class unit at Elementary Flying Training School. Don't misunderstand me, son. I'm not so much passing you as I am passing you forward. You will be someone else's problem. Let someone else decide your fate.

JIMMY: *(taking the form)* Thank you, sir.

PSYCHOLOGY OFFICER: Good luck, Grady. Oh, and for the record, a peregrine is a falcon, not a hawk.

JIMMY: Yes, sir. And sir? For the record, I have never turned an oven on or off in my life.

Jimmy continues his exit. The Psychology Officer exits opposite.

SCENE 5

No.5 Elementary Flying Training School, High River, Alberta. Civilian Flight Instructor Chalmers leads a group of Chipper, two other Leading Air Craftsmen and a straggling Jimmy out to a Tiger Moth on the flight line. All are excited, wearing full flight suits, leather flying caps and parachutes. Jimmy lags behind, walking in great discomfort from the chute straps tightly choking his groin.

CIVILIAN INSTRUCTOR CHALMERS: *(over his shoulder)* You four sprogs will remain in C-Flight until you successfully finish your training here at High River or until you successfully fail. Fair warning: one in four fail Elementary Training. So, if you don't want to take a one-way trip to the washing machine in Trenton, I suggest you start paying attention now!

(he turns and sees Jimmy) Grady! Get your arse up here, now!

The three LACs turn to watch Jimmy.

Whoa! Sunshine! You trying to transfer to the Women's Division?

JIMMY: *(as he tries to jog, the straps choke even more)* No sir.

CIVILIAN INSTRUCTOR CHALMERS: *(shaking his head)* Hold it right there! Now the rest of you, I want you to take a good close look at this man's chute. This is a perfect demonstration of how not to walk out to the Flight Line!

He stands behind Jimmy and pulls up even tighter on the chute straps and peers around. Jimmy stifles a gasp.

Sprog-nuts! Don't ever, ever tighten your chute straps until after you get to the flight line – or you'll end up with a high-pitched pair of sprog-nuts! Got it?

ALL LACs: Yes sir!

CIVILIAN INSTRUCTOR CHALMERS: Got it, Balzac?

He loosens Jimmy's chute straps.

JIMMY: Yes, sir.

CIVILIAN INSTRUCTOR CHALMERS: Now, for all you newcomers to the province of Alberta, you'll be happy to learn that the average temperature is 50 degrees Fahrenheit, year-round. And that's because every day is either zero or a hundred. Now I know you've all got your heads full of information, like this is one of almost twenty training schools in Alberta, and over three-hundred and fifty across the country, yap, yap, yap. But you can forget all that now because I guarantee, if you do not pass your air training here as pilot or aircrew you can forget about seeing any of the other air bases here or anywhere else.

Starting now, your training will progress precisely through the following: Takeoffs, Straight and Level Flying, Gentle Turns, Steep Turns, Climbing and Diving, Stalls and Spins, Engine Failure and Glides, and Landings. You will not move on to the next phase of training until you have proved to your instructor that you are capable of executing the element to his approval and you have his initials in your logbook as proof for your next instructor. Until I have personally signed off on an element in your training book in bright red ink, you will not proceed to the next phase of training. And hopefully, in the end, your number of takeoffs will equal your number of landings.

Falling barometric pressure, wind direction is what?

CHIPPER: *(raising his hand)* Counter-clockwise wind rotation.

CIVILIAN INSTRUCTOR CHALMERS: Good. *(he moves to the aircraft)* Now, gentlemen, I want to give you your first close up look at what you'll be flying in. This little stomach pump is your de Havilland Tiger Moth MK II, a.k.a. the Yellow Peril. *(walking around it)* Only one hundred and twenty some odd horsepower, but more than enough to kill you. For the next month or so, the only thing you need to look for when you're in the sky is somebody else's Yellow Peril.

Now, to review everything they taught you up in Edmonton, *(at the nose)* this is the front, so you'll probably want to be facing this way. *(at the engine)* This is what makes it go, *(at the wing)* this is what keeps it up, *(at the tail)* this is the back... *(at the cockpit)* ...and this, this is where you never, ever, never lose your lunch. As a matter of fact, the first sprog that decides to let loose inside any of my kites will not only clean it up, he will clean up every other upchuck in every other aeroplane on this base for the next month. Is that clear?

ALL LACs: Yes sir!

CIVILIAN INSTRUCTOR CHALMERS: Good. If you happen to find that some part of the aeroplane is not where it ought to be, like say your tail is where your prop should be, make a formal complaint to somebody, anybody, but not to me.

Now, I know you're all probably feeling a little queezy right now. You're worried about going up for the first time – bouncing around up there in the middle of nothing – getting your insides all shook up in the heavy turbulence – trying not to think of that big bowl of putrid, sticky oatmeal you had first thing this morning.

The LACs try not to think about their churning stomachs.

But I don't want you to worry, because it's normal for your gut to feel all sour and the back of your throat to taste all vinegary, especially on your first trip.

And just to help you out, I'm going to let you in on a little secret remedy we professional flyers have developed to get over the rough spots, intestinally speaking. If you think you feel like you won't be able to hold it down and you're really going to spew your guts, what you do is this: take yourself over to the back door of the grub shack and get Cookie to give you...

He pulls out a piece of salt pork on a string

...a nice big, greasy, chunk of salt pork...

Chipper faints and slowly regains consciousness.

Take it back to your bunk, leave it in the sun for an hour or so. Then tie a string around it, good and tight – wrap it around two or three times and then knot it, just like this – pull on it a couple of times to test it... And then put your head back... and swallow it *(he appears to swallow it)* But don't let go of the string. And then... pull it back up by the string, nice and slow, three or four times... *(he appears to pull it up and swallow it repeatedly)* – swallow, pull it up, swallow, pull it up...

The LACs all double over and heave violently.

When your stomach is churning up there on a hot day, just remember, things could be worse – you could be grounded, playing with your salt pork.

Now, any preferences as to who wants to go up first?

Every single LAC eagerly raises his hand.

Good lads. Now let's head you back to the hangar where each and every one of you will prove to me that you know the purpose of every single rivet, every splash of glue, every wire, every strut on your kite. Then, and only then, will I start taking you up. Understood?

The LACs all nod and exit with Civilian Instructor Chalmers.

SCENE 6

Gus, in his chute and flying suit, follows a very agitated Civilian Flight Instructor Reid as he circles a Tiger Moth, doing the pre-flight check. Except where otherwise indicated, Gus speaks to the audience throughout the scene.

GUS: *(aside)* I hate to spoil the best moment of my life, but, well, they look a lot sturdier when you're not up close.

Me and Jimmy were there when the Calgary airfield opened in twenty-nine. I was going on seven, and we watched Freddy McCall dancing all over the sky. I seem to remember he was in a giant, invincible, solid-steel aeroplane, because I thought he'd never get it off the ground, it looked so heavy and downright substantial. Just like at the Calgary Stampede with the poster advertising all its "Passenger-Carrying Aeroplanes!"

An Erk enters to assist with the a/c.

But these! These little rag-wing insects, these Tiger Moths, they're canvas and wood for crying out loud! I mean, if he's not careful, a man could put his foot right through the wing!

The instructor unexpectedly climbs into the aft cockpit and motions Gus to climb into the forward cockpit, the exact reverse of the normal student-aft, instructor-forward positioning.

GUS: Uh, sir? Doesn't the student flyer take the aft cockpit?

CIVILIAN INSTRUCTOR REID: *(sharply)* Look, kid. Do you want to have a discussion or fly?

GUS: Fly! Fly, sir!

CIVILIAN INSTRUCTOR REID: Good.

GUS: *(back to his commentary)* Well, I guess this trip is just a little demo, to see if I want to take a test drive myself. I try not to look too unimpressed – try to look like I'm up on all the gumph.

(to Civilian Instructor 2) Uh, sir? I think the tower just raised the checkered flag. Doesn't that mean bad weather and all flights are scrubbed?

> *The instructor impatiently waves him aboard.*

I guess not.

CIVILIAN INSTRUCTOR REID: We've got plenty of time before that front rolls in. Now get aboard if you're coming aboard!

GUS: *(climbing aboard)* So, we run through the pre-flight check…

CIVILIAN INSTRUCTOR REID: Fuel on. Throttle set. *(shouts)* Clear! Contact!

> *On this signal, the Erk pushes/pulls the heavy propeller around one full rotation. The instructor deploys the ignition and the engine comes to life.*

(shouts) Chalks away, now we pray!

GUS: We start to taxi out…

CIVILIAN INSTRUCTOR REID: *(shouting to Gus)* First lesson, kid. When you're in a tail-wheel aircraft, you obviously can't see a thing ahead of you on the ground. So when we taxi out, we have to do a zig-zag, like this.

> *They zig-zag in the a/c.*

All the way out to the runway. And when you take off, you keep your stick and rudder straight, and sort of watch the edge of the runway out of the corner of your eye. Once the tail comes up, you can see the rest of the way. That should keep you from killing yourself before you start!

> *The instructor briefly revs the engine.*

GUS: *(nodding)* We stop and do a quick run-up on the engine, but she's pretty warm already. Then we start the takeoff, unstick…

The aeroplane comes to level and then lifts up into the air, coming to level flight.

...and up we go. So far, so good. My stomach's getting itself used to the peculiar sensations. My breathing's okay, awful fast, but no hyper-ventilation. Oh, listen to all the flimsy wires! Are they supposed to vibrate that much and whistle in the wind like that?

We're barely out of sight range of the base...

CIVILIAN INSTRUCTOR REID: *(shouting over the Gosport)* Kid, here's the thing. I just got told they won't send me over to fight. I'm stuck here teaching you sprogs. So, I need to get rid of some of my mixed emotions, if you know what I mean. Are you up for something a little more interesting?

GUS: *(he hasn't heard much of the garbled shouting, but he nods and yells back into the Gosport)* Uh, yes sir!

CIVILIAN INSTRUCTOR REID: *(shouting over the Gosport)* There's no point running away from fear, kid. You'll just die tired.

GUS: *(aside)* Ye gods.

CIVILIAN INSTRUCTOR REID: What do you say we find us a piece of unoccupied sky?

GUS: *(to audience)* And he pulls her into a quick dive.

The nose of the aeroplane inclines downward.

We're picking up speed like there's no tomorrow, and then he pulls up, through level, then up again, straight up!

The nose of the aeroplane lifts up, then up again sharply.

And just like that, we're going straight up, into a loop-the-loop! The poor old Moth feels like she must weigh four hundred tons! *(he struggles against the positive G-force)* I start to feel like engine grease – I mean, my eyeballs feel like they're all sliding back towards my ears. And then, suddenly, everything's back to normal, only now I'm completely upside down, floating.

Gus's knees float up toward his chest; he grabs at his harness to make sure it's secure, but realizes what he's doing and gives up.

A little late for that, I guess. *(looking out and beneath {above} him)* It's generally pretty confusing because the sky's under my feet, but the Moth is still right side up.

I'm thinking I might appreciate a little more time to try to figure this out... But then we start plummeting down again.

The nose of the aeroplane lowers again.

(he struggles against the negative G-force) And we go from floating to four hundred tons again. And then we level out, at about two thousand feet, ripping along, at a hundred and seventy knots.

Gus looks back over his shoulder and the Civilian Instructor grins at him. Gus sports a big fake grin and gives a thumbs-up sign.

(aside) Yeah, I see you checking me out, waiting to see how I take it. But I'm fine. I'm just fine.

CIVILIAN INSTRUCTOR REID: *(shouting)* Still with me, kid?

GUS: *(shouting)* Yes sir! And then... *(he half hides his eyes with his hands, peeking through)*

They repeat the motions.

... off we go again to loop-the-loop. *(he's breathing hard, he giggles)* I'm fine! I'm going to make it! I didn't scream, I didn't gray-out *(he shakes his head hard)* – not completely, anyway – and I'm fine! *(surprised)* Curious how, when you're hanging upside down with so many other things to worry about, you don't even think about falling out.

(yelling into the Gosport) How 'bout some snap rolls, sir! *(aside)* What am I saying?

CIVILIAN INSTRUCTOR REID: *(shouting)* Great idea, sprog!

The aeroplane snaps one wing-over rotation, and repeats.

GUS: *(trying not to feel nauseated)* I guess I should be marveling at the capabilities of this little insect, but I've kind of got my mind on other things. Like, maybe ground school isn't so boring after all. Then we swoop down and start beating up on some fence posts in a field.

CIVILIAN INSTRUCTOR REID: *(shouting)* Better lift your feet, kid!

GUS: Oh, I can feel the friggin' wheels rolling over the fence. *(shouting into the Gosport)* Uh, sir, aren't we getting kind of low?

CIVILIAN INSTRUCTOR REID: *(shouting ahead to Gus)* We're not low, the ground's just high! Yee-ha! She's barely got enough power to get her up, but once you give 'er, she's got more than enough power to kill you. You see, kid, this little Moth's easy to fly, but she's not so easy to fly well.

GUS: Finally, we get back to High River, and all in all, I'm feeling altogether dang proud of myself for surviving this little excursion. He greases-one-on, a perfect three-pointer… twice... *(they bounce quite high before final touchdown)*

CIVILIAN INSTRUCTOR REID: *(shouting over the Gosport)* See, that's what two wings will do for you – lots 'n' lots of lift, so lots 'n' lots of bouncing. Remember, kid, a landing's just a controlled crash.

GUS: *(he groans on the bounce)...* and we do our zig-zagging off the runway, finally stop and he shuts her down. *(he checks his body's status)* I'm fine! I feel swell! *(he pokes his fingers into his ears and shakes his head)* My ears are ringing from the wind and the engine, and I think my tonsils may have come loose, but I'm fine!

Both men climb out of the a/c.

CIVILIAN INSTRUCTOR REID: That'll do me for now. Well, sprog, you practice real hard and pretty soon you'll be able to do that and a whole lot more yourself. What do you think?

> *Gus offers his hand, then turns upstage and heaves. They exit opposite one another.*

SCENE 7

> *The Commanding Officer is in his office, holding a file folder and waiting. Jimmy, in his regular uniform and carrying his flying parachute and gear, enters to stand at attention. As a LAC he now has a white flash on the front of his side cap and a propeller patch on the upper arm of each sleeve.*

C.O.: *(without looking at Jimmy)* I'll say this, Grady. It's a first for us here at No.5 High River – for any R.C.A.F. flight school I should expect. *(he fixes on Jimmy)* Let it be the last, understood?

JIMMY: Yes, sir.

C.O.: Where did you come from just now, class or the Flight Line?

JIMMY: I was heading out to the Flight Line, sir.

C.O.: Right. I want you back there the minute you're done. We don't need you holding up the rest of C-Flight.

JIMMY: Yes sir.

> *The C.O. goes to leave, then stops.*

C.O.: *(trying to keep a straight face)* Oh and, Grady...

JIMMY: Yes sir?

C.O.: Good luck.

> *The C.O. leaves the room and Jimmy waits nervously. Shirley enters and rushes to embrace Jimmy.*

SHIRLEY: *(in tears)* Oh, James! James! James!

JIMMY: Mom! What's wrong? What are you doing here?

SHIRLEY: Why didn't you tell me, son?

JIMMY: Mom!

> *He grabs hold of her arms and holds her away from him. She sees his side cap, breaks into renewed sobs and wraps her arms about him again.*

SHIRLEY: Ohhh! My poor, poor baby!

JIMMY: *(again, he holds her away)* Mom! *Mom!* What's going on? What are you doing here? Is something wrong? Is it Dad?

SHIRLEY: *(trying to control her sobbing)* No, of course not! Your father's fine at the hospital... I'm fine, Elizabeth's fine, we're all fine... *(she breaks down again)*... except for you!

JIMMY: Shhhh! Mom! Not so loud! Here, come and sit down.

> *He guides her over to sit in a chair and goes down on one knee.*

Okay, now Mom – deep breath – nice and slow – Okay? You came all the way out here from Calgary?

SHIRLEY: *(nodding)* I took the train – and then I walked from the station. It was a special fare: five dollars and eighty-five cents return. *(she focuses on him and his side cap again)* Oh, why didn't you tell me, James?

JIMMY: Tell you what, Mom?

SHIRLEY: That you... that you...

JIMMY: That I what, Mom?

SHIRLEY: *(she breaks into sobs again)* ...that you had... *(whispers)* ...you know...

JIMMY: What?

SHIRLEY: You know...

JIMMY: What?

SHIRLEY: *(she blurts it out)* The clap!

JIMMY: What?

SHIRLEY: *(she bursts into renewed sobs)* I don't blame you for trying to keep it from us...

JIMMY: *(too loud)* I don't... *(quieter, glancing around)* I don't have the clap! Where did you hear that?

SHIRLEY: *(sniffling)* Grace and I went down to the Strand Theatre to see that new picture, "A Yank in the R.C.A.F." with Tyrone Power. You know how I like him whatever picture he's in. And there was an air force boy there all on his own, and two navy boys were in the next row back – and when the sailors saw the white flash on the other boy's cap, they said... they said... all the infected boys have to wear it! That's how the R.C.A.F. can tell who's got V.D.! *(she breaks down again)*

JIMMY: *(taking off his side cap)* Mom! We all wear this here!

SHIRLEY: *(shrieking)* You've all got V.D.?

JIMMY: No! Mom, it's part of our uniform! As soon as we make it past Initial Training School! It's part of the uniform!

SHIRLEY: But you didn't have it in the picture you sent me when you enlisted!

JIMMY: Mom! That was when I was at the Manning Depot. They give us the uniform and everything – but I was just an Acey Deucy....

SHIRLEY: *(horrified)* What?

JIMMY: I mean Aircraftsman 2nd Class. But once we made the cut and got promoted here to Elementary Flying Training School, we officially became Aircrew in Training. That's what the white flash designates. *(he shows her his upper arm sleeve)* And the prop on my sleeve – it shows I'm a LAC... I mean, a Leading Aircraftsman! That's all it means, honest!

SHIRLEY: Oh, James – why do you have to do the aeroplanes? Your father did the aeroplanes in the Great War, and now just look at him, wasting away at that veterans hospital. All he does is drink. Why can't you do the trucks? Or the boats – you're a good swimmer!

JIMMY: Mom, anybody can join the navy. They'll take any old numb-skull. Same with the army. But you've got to have brains and an education to get into the air force. We've got to know algebra and trigonometry. In the army and navy guys can't even spell those words. Heck, the navy's got such low standards they've got button flies on their bell-bottoms!

SHIRLEY: Really?

JIMMY: Sure. And they have to give their officers double-breasted jackets so's they'll think the extra row of buttons is their officers' pay pinned on them!

SHIRLEY: (chuckling) Go on.

JIMMY: That's what they say!

SHIRLEY: But couldn't you ask the air force to let you work at a desk at headquarters or something?

JIMMY: Mom! Mom, are you listening to me, Mom? *(serious but gentle)* I can fly – do you know what that means? I can go where most guys never even dream of going! I can fly, with the birds! I can leave the ground below and fly so high, the clouds are shed angels' wings!

SHIRLEY: *(sniffling)* But James...

JIMMY: And when the war's over, me and Bet, as soon as we're married, we're going to start up our own aero service company. And you're going to be my very first passenger. And I'm going to take you right up alongside some of those clouds so you can reach out your hand and grab one of them – I promise!

SHIRLEY: Oh, I couldn't!

JIMMY: Shed angels' wings, Mom!

SHIRLEY: You're sure? You're sure you don't have *(whispers)*...V.D.?

JIMMY: I swear in the name of the R.C.A.F. that I do not have V.D.!

SHIRLEY: And Gus, too?

JIMMY: *(he has to think about his answer)* I... um... I swear in the name of the R.C.A.F., *(almost under his breath)* that Gus... has a working knowledge of V.D. I mean, I swear... *(he finds a diplomatic compromise)* ...that Gus is a LAC – I mean, a Leading Aircraftsman, too.

SHIRLEY: You're not just saying this to protect me?

JIMMY: I wouldn't keep anything from you, Mom.

SHIRLEY: *(sobbing with relief)* Oh James!

> *They embrace.*

That nice Officer said I'd feel better if I saw you right away.

JIMMY: *(horrified)* You told the C.O. what you thought the problem was?

SHIRLEY: Well, of course! I had to get to see you! Just imagine what was going through my mind!

JIMMY: *(groaning)* I can imagine what's going through his mind – and through the whole school, right about now.

SHIRLEY: Did I do something I oughtn't?

JIMMY: No, Mom. Not a thing.

> *He hugs her and she kisses him on the cheek, then she dabs her tongue with her hanky and wipes the lipstick off his face.*

Mom!

SHIRLEY: I'll have to explain everything to those navy boys next time I see them...

JIMMY: Mom?

SHIRLEY: Yes, dear?

JIMMY: Me and Gus will take care of the navy.

SHIRLEY: Are you sure?

JIMMY: *(nodding yes)* Just promise me you won't sail home, okay?

SHIRLEY: *(she pulls back, completely serious)* Don't be silly, dear. Don't you know? There's a snowstorm outside! I'll take the train!

> *Jimmy escorts Shirley off as the lights fade.*

SCENE 8

The lights slowly fade to near black, 1:00 a.m. The sound of a large dorm full of boys sleeping, snoring, coughing, sniffling, snorting and sleep-mumbling is heard. These sounds fade out and are replaced by the sound of a dripping shower. The harsh light of a single bulb in the dorm's shower area comes up. A mop stands in the corner.

Gus, in his undershirt and sweatpants, enters sleepily to cross through the light and off to the urinals. After a short pause, Jimmy enters, in his undershirt and sweatpants, carrying two navigation books and a gravestone form.

JIMMY: *(frantically leafing through the books)* No, no, no, no, no! What's my true course go? Not the magnetic, I want the true course! How can I learn navigation in the sky when I can't even navigate the stupid textbooks? Fiddlesticks. I'm dead.

He opens the books on the floor and then stands on his head, trying to hold his legs bent at the hips. He looks as if he were sitting on a chair, upside down.

GUS: *(re-enters)* Balzac, it's the middle of the night, for crying out loud. What are you doing in here?

JIMMY: I'm trying to sort out my Dead Reckoning.

GUS: By standing on your head?

JIMMY: No. Chipper told me about this. It's for strengthening my thigh muscles so's I can keep my feet on the rudder pedals in a no-G invert.

GUS: I had to ask...

JIMMY: It also helps me think. Must be working – my legs are already getting sore and I can feel lots of thoughts running into my head! What are you doing up?

GUS: Couldn't sleep in that giant barn of a dorm. And tonight with the baked beans at dinner, I really needed some fresh air. Generally speaking, I'm almost getting used to all the snoring and the farting, even some guys still whimpering 'cause it's their first time away from home.

JIMMY: So?

GUS: It's the guys lying there sporting big grins that get me worried. *(shuffles a form paper with his foot)* Hey, this is the gravestone form. Haven't you filled it in yet?

JIMMY: No. I got kind of spooked by it.

GUS: Nothing to be afraid of. Just pick one of the sappiest verses your Mom would like. But here's the trick. What you really want to do is make sure you cop it on the best date, to give you the most room for a longer, sappier verse.

JIMMY: What?

GUS: Think about it. You need to cop it on a day between one and nine, and in the month of May – the year is the same, so it's your choice. See? But it's got to be May, one to nine. That way, you use up the least number of chiseled characters in the dreary details, and that gives you more free characters to use in the sappy verse area!

He stares at Gus.

JIMMY: Only you could squeeze out the best in death.

GUS: *(shrugging)* It's a gift. *(he yawns and pushes the books with his foot)* Where the heck did you get these anyway? We're not supposed to cover that sort of advanced stuff until Service Flying School.

JIMMY: Betty lent them to me. I'm starting to really worry I'm not going to solo.

GUS: What? Go on, you're not serious.

JIMMY: It's true. Other guys have already done it, and I'm pushing my instruction hours to the limit.

GUS: So? You'll make it. Besides, I've got more hours than you and I'm nowhere near going up on my own.

JIMMY: Ah, you'll solo alright. But just in case I don't make it within the acceptable hours, I'd rather try for Navigation School than be washed out. And you know I've got barely a fruit fly's brain for science to begin with, so I figured I'd better try to get working on this stuff ahead of time.

GUS: *(shaking his head)* You're a sucker for punishment. Just think of it as dressed-up trig, not science.

JIMMY: Easy for you.

GUS: Okay, where's the flyboy in all this ointment?

JIMMY: *(he groans)* Well, my first true course is three-o-eight degrees...

> *Gus leans against Jimmy's legs, preventing him from righting himself.*

GUS: *(reading)* Three-o-eight degrees less two-four-four degrees to equal sixty-four degrees north of the rhumb course. What have you got for your first magnetic?

JIMMY: "Westerly variation add" fourteen degrees to get three-two-two degrees magnetic. Can I get down now?

GUS: What's your wind?

JIMMY: *(laughs)* My wind? I wouldn't ask that from where you're standing!

GUS: Come on!

JIMMY: Ten thousand feet, blowing at fifty miles an hour from three-four-six degrees. Look, my head's going to pop if you don't let me down.

GUS: *(ignoring Jimmy, he grabs a mop)* Don't worry, there's a mop. And your speed is four hundred miles an hour, right?

JIMMY: Yes.

GUS: So you mark four hundred-mile intervals to determine the E.T.A. at each spot...

JIMMY: The Estimated Time of Arrival? But I'm getting lost with the drift. Can I get down now?

GUS: Let's suppose you fly thirty miles on three-two-two degrees magnetic, and you end up three miles off course. That's six degrees of drift. You can estimate it with ten-degree lines, like this...

> *Gus uses Jimmy's legs and the mop handle to demonstrate his 3-pronged "V-shaped" diagram.*

JIMMY: Gus, I'm getting a charley horse! And where the heck did you learn all this stuff?

GUS: Like you said, Betty let me borrow them one weekend.

JIMMY: One weekend? You learned all this in one weekend?

GUS: *(he yanks Jimmy's legs further apart)* Do you want the answers or not?

JIMMY: Okay, okay. Couldn't I just fly back the three miles to course?

GUS: *(he scoffs)* Sure, and you could have tea with Hitler while you're stooging around! No, all you need to do is double the drift angle *(measuring between leg and mop handle)*, head into the wind, and fly for the time you estimate you've been in error, or for the time it takes to cover thirty miles. That'll bring you back to your true course, and then you head into the wind six degrees to allow for this drift.

> *Jimmy collapses onto Gus and they both end up on the floor*

JIMMY: Couldn't I just pick out two objects on the ground and on the map, about thirty miles apart and then just take a compass reading?

GUS: Well sure, but not if there's thick fog – *(indicating Jimmy's posterior on the top of the map)* – or your own broad beam covering the view!

JIMMY: *(shoving Gus)* It's ironic, you know.

GUS: What?

JIMMY: Out of the four of us, Betty and Graziano are the two best pilots – and the air force won't let either of them fly.

GUS: Yeah. Makes you think alright. *(getting excited)* Hey! Want to try making a Mercator chart?

JIMMY: What are you, the Met man now?

GUS: *(grabs a pencil and begins drawing)* Look, you draw the meridians parallel to each other – any scale you want, it doesn't matter – and draw a hypotenuse between them, inclined at the average latitude of the first two parallels of latitude you want to draw. So let's say forty degrees thirty feet is the angle, and the distance A-to-B measured along the hypotenuse is the distance between parallels forty degrees and forty-one degrees.

> *Jimmy stares at Gus.*

Then you divide each of the borders of the chart into sixty equal sections... *(he looks up at Jimmy)...* so you get the distortion of the parallels of latitude... *(trailing off)* What?

JIMMY: *(shaking his head)* Rusky, what the hell are you doing?

GUS: What? You wanted help, didn't you?

JIMMY: But if you get too good at this stuff they'll ship you off to be a navigation instructor and you'll never see action!

GUS: Oh. *(he drops the pencil and gets up)* Okay, well, forget I said anything. I just got up to take a leak. *(he grabs the mop and leaves)*

JIMMY: Wait! *(he gathers up all the books and charts)* I'm dead reckoning, Gus, I reckon I'm dead!

Jimmy picks up his books and runs after Gus.

SCENE 9

A series of Tiger Moths is heard taking off, one after the other. As the last one flies off, the sound fades.

A Tiger Moth is heard until Jimmy, in his flying suit and gear, climbs aboard the aft cockpit. Civilian Instructor Chalmers is in the forward cockpit.

CIVILIAN INSTRUCTOR CHALMERS: Don't mind me. We instructors just go along to find out where the crash site will be.

JIMMY: *(performing the actions)* Seven thousand feet. I ease back on the throttle *(he reduces the throttle sharply)*, right back to idle, then I nudge her nose up *(he yanks back on the stick)* and keep her just above the horizon...

And then, then there's nothing. We stall, and I bring her nose up even more, and then give her full left rudder. Over we roll, and down we go – round and round...

The aircraft begins to spin.

It's kind of hypnotic at first. But then you start to notice the little things, like the fact that the altimeter's spinning itself off the dial. And there's a lot of details on the ground that are starting to come into focus mighty rapidly.

It's a lot like spinning out our old Mercury coupe out on the ice on Chestermere Lake. You want to slam on your brakes and hope the car will eventually run out of oomph and stop.

Here we are, plummeting headlong to the ground, *(he laughs nervously)* pretty much out of control. And every inch of me just wants to raw back on the stick and yank her nose up – but that's the worst thing you can do because that will just make your spin worse. No, first, you've got to give her full opposite rudder, and then you've got to push her nose down – and this feels about as smart as giving the devil a tip for holding the gate open for you, but you have to do it, to reduce your angle of attack. And you think you've done the exact wrong thing because now you're spinning even faster *(the spinning is faster)*. But you've just got to trust it, nice and easy... *(he rams the stick forward)* And sure enough, she'll stop.

The aircraft violently inclines forward a bit more.

So now you're just plummeting straight down, so you've just got to give her her head, gently... *(he yanks the stick back)* ...and up she comes, nice and easy, and you level out at a comfortable level. *(he jerks the plane violently, over-correcting, first too high, then side to side)*

CIVILIAN INSTRUCTOR CHALMERS: *(yelling over the Gosport)* You crazy prune! What the hell are you trying to do, kill us both? You don't take a spin all the way down until you hit China! For any aerobatics, and especially spins, you've got to leave a cushion of three thousand feet, beneath you, not above! Check your altimeter!

JIMMY: I've got us at four thousand, Sir.

CIVILIAN INSTRUCTOR CHALMERS: And what's the altitude of Calgary and area?

JIMMY: Three thousand, five hundred feet... *(he trails off as he realizes what he is saying)*

CIVILIAN INSTRUCTOR CHALMERS: Which puts us at five hundred feet above the ground! You're so low I can see up that cow's behind, for corn's sake! Now climb back up!

*Jimmy is horrified and blanches when he looks out at the ground.
The Moth climbs back up.*

JIMMY: *(aside, repeatedly batting the side of his head)* I was just testing to see if he was paying attention...

CIVILIAN INSTRUCTOR CHALMERS: *(yells over the Gosport)* What did you say?

JIMMY: Nothing, sir!

CIVILIAN INSTRUCTOR CHALMERS: Now let's get this straight – when I've got control, I can fly as low as this thing will go. I can fly inside the damn cow if I want! But you and all the rest of you pimply little ham-fisted, prune sprogs will not venture below three thousand feet Above Ground Level unless you're landing. And even then, I'd prefer it if you pancaked with a thousand feet to spare! Now get this thing landed before I die of heart failure! Or old age! Or which ever comes first! *(he pulls out a bottle of Milk of Magnesia and takes a big swig)* There's old pilots and bold pilots, but there's no old, bold pilots. And then there's just jerks who shouldn't get anywhere near a kite in the first place!

JIMMY: *(he knocks the side of his head with his hand. Aside, even louder)* One of the fortunate side-effects of spinning so fast from so high is the air pressure in your ears makes you temporarily deaf!

The lights go down and they exit, flying off.

SCENE 10

The sound of a Tiger Moth flying slowly overhead, landing and taxiing is heard. Gus, in the rear cockpit, is riding motionless in a Tiger Moth as it zig-zag taxies into dispersal. During the flying lesson, Gus has vomited into his glove, trying to hide the fact from the Chief Flying Instructor. The C.F.I. in the forward cockpit shuts down and climbs out of the aircraft.

C.F.I.: Son, I'm going to be straight with you. This airsickness, you should have been able to beat it by now.

GUS: *(hiding his full glove)* But it's getting better, sir. I didn't even feel ill this trip!

C.F.I.: *(nodding towards his glove)* I could see you spewing behind me, son, in there and on your boots, and more than once. You just can't have that when you're in control of a kite. I've known a lot of guys with the same problem, but what's usual is, they get over it pretty quick. Even the worst cases eventually get it to stop. But this has been too long, and I just can't sign-off on your training when you can't make a single circuit without the airsickness. Do you understand?

GUS: *(quietly)* Yes, sir.

C.F.I.: It's a shame because if it wasn't for this problem, you'd probably make a fair pilot. But it's time to stop kidding ourselves.

GUS: You're not washing me out are you? Please don't! I'll do anything, anything!

C.F.I.: Standard procedure says I should.

GUS: I'll do anything!

C.F.I.: Every single time you go up, so does your lunch, and that sort of thing doesn't instill confidence – not to mention when you're busy spewing, your flight controls aren't a priority. And I won't have you otherwise occupied, not in the middle of the war, not when there's others depending on you. I don't understand it, because your record shows you were excellent on the Link trainer back at I.T.S.

GUS: *(dejected)* My record also shows that I keep a good kit 'cause my bunk sheets are tighter than a sparrow's behind.

C.F.I.: But the Link simulator is firmly attached to the floor, not thousands of feet up in the air. You just can't handle being in control of the kite.

GUS: I can ask the Medical Officer to give me something.

C.F.I.: All the *Milk of Magnesia* in the world isn't enough to get you your wings. Or keep my instructors trying to get you your wings.

GUS: But sir...

C.F.I.: Settle down, Minton. Just because you can't fly, doesn't mean you can't be useful in other ways. You've had abysmal grades in all aspects of your flying and ground school classes, except for math and navigation. There your skills are impressive. The best we've ever seen here at No.5. Your test scores are remarkable, right through the roof, as a matter of fact. But you just can't take operating the real thing.

GUS: *(quietly)* I was just always pretty good with numbers and stuff.

C.F.I.: Well, the air force definitely has a place for that sort of thing. *(he considers his idea)* Listen, son – what I'd like to try to do is transfer your training over to navigation. I know Wop May, the C.O. up at No.2 Air Observer School, Edmonton, and he owes me one from our barnstorming days. Let me go give him a call and see if I can talk him into taking you on.

GUS: *(relieved)* So, I won't be washed-out?

C.F.I.: If I can swing it, no.

GUS: *(disappointed)* Navigation.

C.F.I.: Look, kid, I know how bad you want your wings, but it just isn't going to happen. Hell, be serious – you're upchucking so hard you're going to start leaking from the other end soon, and you wouldn't want to dump your sump all over a nice Spitfire, now would you? I know navigation's not what you hoped for, but think about it. You may not be at the actual controls, but you'll be able to guide a bomber from London all the way up a German dog's arse!

GUS: Edmonton.

C.F.I.: It won't be easy – you'll have to work your rudder off to catch up to the rest of the class. We need you, kid. You'll have a great future as a navigator. I guarantee it. In fact, you'll probably be offered a commission when you graduate.

GUS: Yes, sir. But can you be sure I'll get overseas?

C.F.I.: Between you, me and the lamp post, the only thing you want to watch out for is being too good. Regardless of knowing the right answers, you don't want to be seen as too good, otherwise they'll saddle you up with a damned instructor's certificate and...

GUS: ...I'd be stuck here teaching idiot kids and miss the whole war, like...

C.F.I.: Like me?

GUS: No, sir!

C.F.I.: You just remember not to be as goldarn smart-arsed as I know you are, and you won't end up a poor sap like me and my civilian instructors, chained like dogs to Canada and sure to meet our deaths at the hands of scared little untalented sprogs in flaming Tiger Moths.

GUS: Yes, sir.

C.F.I.: You won't regret this. And you won't have to worry about losing your lunch every time you take off. You wait here and I'll make the call. Then I'll get the Duty Officer to start the paperwork.

GUS: Sir?

C.F.I.: Yes?

GUS: Won't it just look like I couldn't cut it, flying ability-wise?

C.F.I.: I'll personally write a letter outlining nothing but your excellent navigator prospects, nothing negative; you have my word. *(he extends* *his hand to Gus)* But if you shake my hand with that glove full of puke, I will send you to Trenton! Now wait here.

They shake hands and the C.F.I. exits. Gus slowly unbuckles his chute with one hand, while still holding his glove of vomit. Jimmy runs in, checking over his shoulder. He is wearing the accessories of every newly soloed pilot: a white silk scarf with dark blue polka-dots and a pair of Tone-Ray aviator sunglasses. In his utter joy, Jimmy does not notice Gus's mood or plight.

JIMMY: Rusky! Hey! I did it! I did it!

GUS: *(sees Jimmy's scarf and sunglasses)* You soloed?

JIMMY: I did! I did! Finally! I thought I'd never make it, but finally I soloed!

GUS: You brat! So, give. What was it like?

JIMMY: Your first solo flight. Oh I can't tell you! It was amazing, and routine, all at once. I mean, all the training, all the hours of instruction and going over everything over and over – and suddenly, there I was, heading along the asphalt! And the second she took air, I could feel the exact second, and there we were, me and my Moth! And the higher we went, the better it got. And then I started giggling like a school girl – I did, really! I checked that there wasn't anyone with me, 'cause I couldn't hardly believe it all, and it was just me, so I started shouting and laughing and flying like a bird! It was... I just don't know how to describe it, it's such a wonderful feeling, the sensation! *(he spins with his arms outstretched)*

It was a lot like riding horseback. That always made me feel like we were flying – ha! Riding feels like flying, and flying feels like riding! I mean, you and the horse are one together, working together, depending on one another... and soaring! Only this was better than any fence I ever jumped on back of a nag. All of a sudden, I could feel everything, not just, you know, work it through my head. This time, I strapped her on and I could feel everything we were doing. And oh, boy, it was like the whole wide unoccupied sky belonged to me. I could've flown right into the Sheep River and back out again, without getting wet, it was so great!

And all the instruments! You know how murderous it was, trying to remember them: airspeed, turn indicator, altimeter, tachometer, gyro, left to right, left to right – how it made you look at them all jumpy and jaggy. Well, as soon as I was up there all on my lonesome, it wasn't... you know... it wasn't by rote any more. Well, okay, I mean it was by rote, it always will be, like they drummed it into our heads. But this time, it was like magic. It became one smooth and natural motion, like peanut butter crust to crust, like just spreading your eyes over the whole lot of them all at once, automatically, like you've done it a thousand times – like when we first felt our hands relax on the stick and go from hard ham-fists to easy control of the reins. Her creaks and groans, all of her buzzing wires and struts, and the slight rippling of her canvas, and the blur of the prop, everything just came together to sound like some beautiful new song. Everything, the wind even – suddenly, the wind, it didn't sting any more. Suddenly, it turned into a terrific breeze, keeping me cool under the glaring sun!

And then the two of you, you circle round and join the circuit, easing on in back to earth, you and the kite, working together, feeling that beautiful flare, holding it, holding it, and then settling down, barely touching – I swear, I could feel when the very first rubber fibre of her tires snugged onto the earth, so soft and easy, like the first ray of dawn swathing your cheek in the morning...

GUS: You thumped her down hard, didn't you?

JIMMY: Yeah, I hit like an anvil and bounced twice. Oh, but Rusky, that sensation, of finally being fully in control, being one with her, just you and Lady Moth, painting the sky together, touching...

GUS: ...touching shed angels' wings. *(trying to be glad)* I get it; it was good. Congratulations.

JIMMY: Thanks. *(posing with his hand on his sunglasses)* How do you like the Tone-Rays?

The sound of the classmates who have been chasing Jimmy gets closer, and he quickly checks around and behind him.

56

GUS: *(monotone)* Great. And why the hell are you so jumpy?

JIMMY: Those guys are trying to toss me into the water tank – you know, the rights of passage for soloing, and all that... *(he stops and looks at Gus)* What's up with you? Your face is so long they'd have to continue it on page two in the newspaper.

GUS: *(quietly)* I had to go up with the C.F.I..

JIMMY: *(very serious)* Jeeze, Gus. How did it go?

GUS: The Chief Flying Instructor has informed me that I'm not going to get my wings.

JIMMY: Not "L.M.F.?"

GUS: I don't have a "lack of moral fibre." What I've got is a lack of puke control.

JIMMY: Oh, Gus.

GUS: *(holding up his glove full of vomit)* I tried to control it. I tried with all my might. But I just couldn't control it. I tried. I did. But I just couldn't do it. I couldn't even hide it.

JIMMY: *(forced levity)* So that's why you've been visiting the dry cleaners so often – and we just thought you were a natty dresser!

GUS: You think you had problems. I couldn't solo by the ten hours – twelve hours, fifteen, even. I just couldn't do it. I just ran out of time. And then I had to go up with the C.F.I., and I was still spewing my guts out. So, it's scrub-time as far as pilot training goes for me.

JIMMY: But you were always fine in the beginning, when the instructors were taking us up and they had the controls.

GUS: I know, that's the problem. Most guys get pukey when they're just riding along, and once they're in control, they're fine. With me, it's because of the exact opposite. I guess it's the pressure. Give me anything to do in a kite, just don't make me take control of her.

JIMMY: Gus. I'm sorry...

GUS: He's going to send me up to Edmonton, to No.2, Air Observers. Better than getting washed-out.

Jimmy's classmates enter en masse, shouting "there he is," "get him," etc. and grab him.

JIMMY: *(calling back to Gus)* Uh, let's go into town and get loaded tonight. We can still fly together. I'll fly and you'll be my navigator!

Gus gives a thumbs-up sign, and the classmates grab Jimmy, shoving and dragging him off for the ritual dousing. The C.F.I. returns, carrying an envelope.

C.F.I.: It's all set, Minton. Take this and give it to the C.O. when you get there. I'll get the Duty Officer here to notify theirs up north.

GUS: *(taking the paper)* Yes, sir.

C.F.I.: Stick with it, and don't you make me look bad, alright?

GUS: Yes, sir.

Gus exchanges a salute with the Chief Flying Instructor and they exit separate ways.

SCENE 11

The remaining classmates re-enter, anxiously awaiting the announcement of their E.F.T.S. graduation. Jimmy joins the rest of the remaining LACs and marches to centre stage to stand at attention. As the Corporal calls out the names, the LACs salute and then march out, left to flying training, right to other aircrew training.

CORPORAL: LAC Miller, Jackson R., S.R.8639.

LAC: Sir!

CORPORAL: Bomber and Air Gunner, No.8, Lethbridge.

> *The disappointed LAC exits to the right.*

LAC Ellis, Clarence G., S.V.31248.

LAC: Sir!

CORPORAL: Trenton.

> *The stunned LAC exits up centre.*

JIMMY: *(under his breath)* S.F.T.S.... Please let it be pilot training. Please, S.F.T.S....

CORPORAL: LAC Grady, James E., R.U.27433.

JIMMY: Sir!

CORPORAL: Pilot. No.3 Service Flying Training School, Calgary.

> *Jimmy turns and marches off, smiling.*

SCENE 12

> *No.3 Flying Training School, Calgary. Jimmy is in the forward cockpit of a Harvard. His R.C.A.F. Instructor is in the aft cockpit.*

JIMMY: Tell you something you won't see in any picture show newsreel. One of the first things you get introduced to in the cockpit – any plane – Tiger Moths, Harvards – doesn't matter.

They all got... well, it's a... a kind of... Well, it's a piss pipe, is what it is. You know, so's a guy can let go if he has to. I mean it's not like you can pull over to the side of a cloud. It empties right out the bottom of the fuselage, usually out of a fancy looking pipe. You'd think it was some kind of sophisticated mechanism, sticking out of the aircraft like that... Well, I guess it is kind of vital!

Problem is, the flying hours are so short, even the long haul training, you know, cross-country and all that – well, none of us ever gets a chance to figure out how to use the piss pipe before we go off to solo. And with each new aircraft, sometimes you can't work out where it is or sometimes even what it looks like.

Now, me and my instructor are finishing up what I'm thinking is a none-too-stellar effort on my part *(he nods toward the aft cockpit)* and I'm thinking the two of us are going to be dating in this bird for a lot more hours yet. So I prepare for landing just like the textbook: check trim, mixture, pitch, fuel, flaps, gear and gyros.

... and I bring us down in that Harvard just as pretty as the press in his pants. We both throw open the canopies and just as I zig-zag off and bring us in to the Flight Line...

> *As the plane approaches, the engine noise comes to full volume to idle speed.*

R.C.A.F. INSTRUCTOR: *(climbing out of the aft cockpit, yelling above the engine noise)* You're doing alright, kid! Go on! Swing her round, re-trim and take her right back up! She's all yours!

> *The instructor slaps Jimmy on the shoulder, slams the aft canopy shut, and exchanges a thumbs-up with him. He then jumps down from the wing and runs clear of the plane, to join Betty and a group of other interested LACs.*

JIMMY: Solo! Holy jumping! First in my class this time! All the guys are crowding around to watch! My heart's thumping so hard, I could spit!

So I rev her good and hard, to make sure I've got everyone's attention, and then I shut my canopy.

The crowd moves away to exit.

And I zig-zag taxi back out, 'til I get to the exact centre of the runway...

The engine volume revs to taxi. A green light flashes.

They clear me and give me the green right off. I re-trim and reset the mixture to rich, and I keep my feet on the brakes just to give a better show, give her full throttle and she's straining to get loose...

The engine roars to full take-off speed.

And... I unstick!

The engine noise fades to a low volume of normal flight. He adjusts the controls with his left hand.

Gear up, retract flaps, and I'm soaring like a frigging bird, solo! Six hundred and twenty-five horsepower and she's all mine. Ho-hooo!

He suddenly realizes his bladder is full.

Ohhh jeeze! I gotta go! I had to take a leak when we landed, but I didn't want to say anything and get him browned off. Oh jeeze! I've got to go so bad my back teeth are floating! What'll I do? I can't hold it! I'm going to wet my pants! Oh jeeze... Wait! The piss-pipe! Where's the piss-pipe? There!

He fumbles for the pipe with his left hand and his right hand allows the stick to go forward, dipping the nose.

Whoa, jeeze, keep her nose up, man! Straight and gently climbing. Everybody's looking. Keep her straight and gently climbing!

Oh jeeze! I'm going to burst! C'mon, c'mon, c'mon! Oh, jeeze, it's like overalls, the zipper opens up, not down... I've never been left-handed! Oh jeeze! C'mon! Look, I am not climbing out of this bird with a wet monkey suit! Okay, there, I'm in... Jeeze, I don't remember it being so small. Oh, well, the vent's letting in mighty cold air, that's why...

61

At last he connects the pipe, concentrates hard for a moment, and then begins to relieve himself.

Ohhh! Oh thank you! Thank you, lord! Oh, thank you! Oh...

The lights cross-fade to Shirley, carrying a basket of wet sheets, going into her yard to hang out the washing on the line. A Harvard soars low overhead.

SHIRLEY: *(she stops abruptly as she feels something wet fall on her head and the sheets)* Land's sakes! Can you beat that! They never show that on the newsreels. They're all bright yellow, but now I'm not so sure it's yellow paint. As if flushing latrines on the CPR tracks wasn't bad enough! Now every time I do a laundry, I get smart-alecky flyboys buzzing overhead, piddling on my wash!

Shirley exits quickly. The lights fade.

SCENE 13

The light dims to a low light in a room off the hangar with black night beyond. Chipper, Jimmy and the two other LACs in C-Flight are in their flying kit trying to stay awake for their turn at night flying training.

CHIPPER: *(anxiously checking the weather)* Jeeze. Why don't the instructors cancel? There's too much weather coming in too fast. Those are towering cumulus building up – even I can see that. It's just not good. I mean I know they've got to stick to the schedule when it comes to night flying, but I'd rather lose a night than lose my sorry backside getting slammed in a downdraft.

He hears an approaching Harvard.

Finally. Well let's just get back, get up and get this over with. *(the aircraft engine is struggling)* Shit! *(he runs to scan the darkness outside)*

> *Silence. There is a sudden crash and the light of an explosion illuminates his face.*

(yelling) Fire! Fire! Call the crash truck, the meat wagon! Fire! Fire!

> *They all rush off into the dark toward the crash.*

SCENE 14

> *A cold November Saturday, downtown Calgary, outside a butcher shop. Shirley is laden with shopping packages, heading for the door of the shop. An inebriated Hillis is dressed in his black Royal Australian Air Force uniform with his newly acquired "BA" on his chest and a small bottle of brandy in his pocket. He has just relieved himself in the alley and, as he concentrates on closing his fly, he patrols the shop front. The cuffs at the bottom of his trouser legs have been undone. He and Shirley collide.*

SHIRLEY: Oh! *(her packages fall to the ground)*

HILLIS: Beg your pardon, Missus. I just got caught short. Oh, but aren't you the right little Sheilagh! *(he tries to gather the packages but ends up sprawling on the ground)*

SHIRLEY: What? Young man, you're drunk!

HILLIS: Why yes. Yes, I am. Drunk as a... what is that thing you have here? It's kinda like a wombat in a tuxedo...

SHIRLEY: Good lord, you stink of liquor!

HILLIS: Stink, stunk? Skunk! Drunk as a skunk! Yes, Missus, guilty as charged! *(singsong)* One's alright, two's the most, three's under the table, and four's under the host! Oh, I am lit up like a switchboard on Christmas day!

SHIRLEY: I've a mind to report you to your commanding officer!

HILLIS: *(seriously, pleading)* No, no, please Missus! Don't do that, please! It's not my fault, honest!

SHIRLEY: My boy's going to be a pilot, and he'd never let himself be seen in your condition. Buck up, for heaven's sake.

HILLIS: *(he snaps to attention, slightly swaying)* Flight Sergeant Harold K. Hillis, best bloody Bomb Aimer/Nose Gunner in all of No.8 Bombing and Gunnery School, Lethbridge. *(firing two imaginary air guns)* A-a-a-a-a-a-a! I aims to please! *(looking down at his open fly)* Well, I tries to aims to please... *(he stuffs his shorts and shirt back in, closes the zipper and then holds out his hand to shake hands)*...but you can call me Harry! I'm a better bomb aimer. I can drop a fully armed cookie from five thousand feet right down a lady's brassiere! Not that I'd ever want to explode a lovely woman's undergarments, you understand. Let me put it a little less personal – I can drop a bomb down a chimney without getting soot on the fins! *(loud whisper)* You know, the only difference between peace and war is where the bombs fall.

I am also quite efficient in the art of deflection shooting – you know, firing just ahead of the target so the bullets hit him when he gets there? It's also called leading. And I owe it all to pissing – see, every time I piss, I aims my peter...

SHIRLEY: *(horrified)* Young man!

HILLIS: Oh, well, maybe that's a little too technical for a lady such as yourself. *(he changes the subject)* See, Missus, as for my current state, it was my mates who got me tanked up, to celebrate our graduation, see, in our local hang out. Afterwards, when it was closing time, the barkeep told me to clear the dirty glasses and put away the unused liquor. So far, I've put away an extra three bottles. And then... well I sort of don't remember quite what happened next, but all of a sudden, I come to and find myself here, without my mates and worse, without me trouser cuffs! Imagine! I've got this natty black Royal Australian Air Force uniform that all the girls just love to touch, and here they've gone and undone my trouser cuffs! *(wistfully)* Oh, and wasn't they some fair pair of terrific trouser cuffs, too. "Tailored especially for A/G Hillis, December thirteen, nineteen-hundred and forty-two, Town Hall Shop, Lethbridge." I remember them like it was yesterday.

SHIRLEY: Even so, it's barely one o'clock in the afternoon.

HILLIS: I know I've had a few, and I also know how few I've had.

SHIRLEY: It's wonderful that you've signed up, knowing you may have come all this way, god forbid to die...

HILLIS: What? No, Missus! I didn't just come to Canada today! Cracky, it took us weeks to get here from down under.

SHIRLEY: *(confused)* Today? What? No, I meant... never mind. I won't report you, but you should be more careful in the future!

HILLIS: Oh, bless you, Missus!

SHIRLEY: *(she's ready to enter the butcher shop, but he blocks her way)* Now, excuse me, please, I want to go into this shop.

HILLIS: *(he blocks her)* Oh, no, Missus! Until I come face to fly with my trouser cuffs, I'm doing my bit by enforcing the wartime regulations of this establishment – keeping lovely ladies such as yourself out. You don't dare go in this shop, Missus! Not on this day!

SHIRLEY: I want to go into the butcher shop.

HILLIS: *(hushed)* Read the sign, Missus.

SHIRLEY: What are you talking about? Let me past.

HILLIS: It's Saturday, Missus! And the sign plainly says you cannot go in!

SHIRLEY: What? What do you mean?

HILLIS: *(reciting the sign)* "Ladies, don't bring your fat cans in here on Saturdays." Now, that's the butcher talking, not me. I'd have been a little more subtle if it was me.

SHIRLEY: But I don't have a fat can today.

HILLIS: Oh, I know, Missus. We all like to feel that way some days. And a lady's will is always bigger than a fella's won't. *(sensitively)* I'd have been more delicate about it myself.

SHIRLEY: What? Oh, for heaven's sakes! It's fat cans, not fat cans!

HILLIS: No matter how you says it, they don't want you in there when it's a busy Saturday. Too many fat cans in there and before you know it, there's more flesh than meat!

SHIRLEY: Oh, you idiot! Fat cans are the cans we have in the kitchen to collect fat, meat drippings – to make explosives and glue! To help win the war? You know: "We shouldn't throw it out, we should throw it at Hitler!"

HILLIS: *(singsong)* Use it up, wear it out, make it do, or do without!

SHIRLEY: Yes, yes, that's right. But as for fat cans...

HILLIS: *(sensitively)* Like I said, if it was up to me, I would've been a little less abrasive and had the sign read "keesters" or "rears" – anything but fat cans!

SHIRLEY: Good Lord. Fat cans – I mean, fat cans, does not refer to ladies' bottoms! It's drippings! Cans of meat drippings!

HILLIS: No! You mean, it's buckets of grease? Not broad-beamed Sheilaghs?

SHIRLEY: No! And won't you know it when your aeroplane doesn't fall to pieces for lack of glue one day, all because enough of us ladies were diligent enough to look after our fat cans – I mean, fat cans!

HILLIS: *(apologetically, offering his bottle)* Oh, beg your pardon, Missus.

I didn't mean to offend. Here, have yourself a bang old swig! Genuine Emu Brandy, all the way from Adelaide. The golden champagne of Australian brandies!

They shuffle about, he still getting in the way of her entering the shop.

SHIRLEY: *(refusing the offer)* I'd almost shake the devil's hand before I'd touch that. I hope no one else sees you in this condition.

HILLIS: You think this is bad, you should have seen me when my Lethbridge mates had me strap on ice skates for hooky.

SHIRLEY: Hockey.

HILLIS: Call it what you like, but all I know is it got me more wobbled up and woozy than any ride in a kite ever did. *(he remembers his cold crotch)* And these Canadian boys with their snow. I got my privates so frozen it nearly changed my voice back up!

SHIRLEY: *(checking her watch)* Oh now I won't have time to go into the shop if I want to make it to visiting hours at the hospital.

HILLIS: *(confused again)* Ah, but see, that's just as well, 'cause anyway, it's Saturday and they don't want your fat can in there!

SHIRLEY: It's a fat can, for heaven's sake! Fat can, fat can, fat can! And I don't have one today!

HILLIS: *(he slaps her backside)* I know, Missus! You've probably got a fair dinkum caboose most days, but not today! No fat cans on a Saturday!

SHIRLEY: *(exasperated)* For the last time, it's a fat can, not a fat can! And I don't have one! Oh, never mind. I've had enough. I'll just have to do without and come back next week.

She gathers up her packages and begins to exit.

I hope you're good at what you've been trained to do, young man. I almost pity the enemy, because if aggravation wins wars, you'll surely send the Germans running! And in the future, you'd be better off drinking Canada Dry!

Shirley exits. Hillis staggers after her.

HILLIS: *(shouting after her)* I'm bloody well trying to drink Canada dry, Missus. But it's some big bloody country – it's going to take me a little time to finish the job!

Hillis staggers out.

SCENE 15

Jimmy is flying alone aboard a Harvard trainer, in the dark of night. He looks casually from side to side, appearing to be completely confident and perfectly in control – he continues this in silence for a while.

JIMMY: *(looking straight ahead, in a very controlled and confident voice)* I have no idea where I am.

Cross-country. Cross-country sounds perfectly reasonable, when you have a road. But cross-country when you hardly know where the cross goes across the country, it's damn near impossible. Well, okay, if you're a wiz-bang mathematician navigator like Gus, it's a piece of cake. But me? Jeeze, some nights I get lost just going out to the john! And I can't hardly even pick out bodies of water, or even mountains – it's all just like trying to see fruit flies on black velvet.

I sort of got a handle on the beam exercises.

He activates a switch and the sound of a beeping radio signal sounding like "dit-DAH" is heard.

It's all in Morse Code of course, and you've got your "A" beam on your left. *(listening)* That's right, the "dit-DAH" is "A."

He angles the Harvard to his right. The sound switches to a beeping radio signal sounding like "EN-dit."

And your "N" beam is on your right. *(listening)* That's it, the "EN-dit" is "N" – that's my personal trick for remembering: "EN-dit" just has to be the "N" beam. Both beams are about three degrees wide, and the further you fly adrift of them, the louder the signal. This is all correct for flying towards your beacon; if you're flying from your beacon, it's all opposite.

There's broadcast beacons located every two hundred miles or so, and the theory has it that a pilot can follow these signals from beacon to beacon and get exactly where he's going without so much as a ruffle of his wings. And if you're perfectly on course, those obnoxious beeps merge into one continuous, hypnotic tone. *(the beeps merge into one continuous tone)* And when you're flying that perfect course, you'll fly right over the beacon, in which case *(the tone stops abruptly)* you won't hear anything at all. That's something the air force glowingly refers to as the Cone of Silence.

Anyway, that's the theory. My experience of successfully maintaining my kite perfectly on the beam is pretty well dismal. I mean, it's so mighty touchy, and just the slightest pressure on the stick too much to one side or the other, and you're off. *(as he goes from one side to the other, the appropriate beam signals sound)* Then you try to fix it, but you over-correct, then back too far the other way, trying to get just the right spot. Jeeze Louise! It's harder than dotting an "I" in yellow snow!

It's just so frigging confusing. And if your radio goes on the fritz, *(his radio beeps degenerate into thick static)* it can beep for all it's worth, but it won't get you where you ought to be. Aw, to heck with it. All I want to do is get back to base, if I can find it. I'll take any base, for that matter. Where's Gus when I need him? *(he switches off the radio)*

I heard a guy from No.15 Claresholm got so lost he ended up flying due south, right across the U.S. border. All hell broke loose, when he did, of course. It took forever, but finally it was all sorted out – 'cept by law he wasn't allowed to fly back across the border. So they had to go interrupt a farmer in his field and get him to hitch up his horses and they hauled the Harvard by her tail wheel back some fifty feet into Canada. That was the most international traveling the kid ever got. Word has it just a few weeks later he was on formation training and when he went to move from right-wing to left-wing, he broke the cardinal rule: the aeroplane that is changing position always, always, goes under the leader, so's he can maintain visual contact. This poor guy went over the leader, couldn't see a thing of course, and slammed straight into the other kite. Both souls dead, plus one farmer on the ground.

(he shudders and shakes his head vigorously out of those sobering thoughts) Anyway, I'm still lost here, so let's opt for that wonderful airman's old faithful navigational aid: the Iron Beam! *(he sees the railroad track and dives down quickly)* I take her right down to the deck about 90 feet high, where I can pick up the visual, and I travel in style along the good old trustworthy Canadian Pacific Railway! Yes siree, when they built railways, they always made them go someplace, and all a flyboy's got to do is follow along until he gets where it's going. I can cook my logs when I get back, so's there's no mention of irregularities in my navigational skills. When you're lost at night out here on the prairies, you can always find a railway and a railway will always take you home – maybe not to your home, but it will definitely take you to somebody's home. Just follow the... shit!

He instantly turns himself and his a/c to a hard left, vertical orientation, so that the a/c's port wing is lowest to the ground, perpendicularly.

(gasping) Grain elevator!

He recovers to straight and level flying.

(recovering) Alberta Wheat Pool – one of the biggest predators of aircrews anywhere in the country. If you're going to fly the C.P.R. iron beam, you've got to watch out for the grain elevators. I remember High River had five of them. You can suffocate if you fall in to one when it's full of grain. It's the dust. It happens all the time, even to the most experienced farmers. It's a pretty gruesome way to go. And all

that grain dust will catch fire at the drop of a hat, so you definitely don't want to fly your kite into one. *(he chuckles)* Ha! The dust will choke you, but the fire will fry you – now that's a real air force approach! "It will kill you" and "It will kill you." Perfect!

(he adjusts the nose of the Harvard slightly downward) One thing you've got to watch for though, you've got to pay attention to the lay of the land, in case the elevation increases and the aeroplane doesn't, because the other hazard when you're flying the iron beam is the occasional... shit!

> *A very bright oncoming train light blinds him and its whistle blows then fades as he frantically pulls the a/c up to clear an oncoming steam engine.*

Trains! The other hazard is trains. *(squirming slightly in his seat)* And all the piss-pipes in the world won't help when there's a ten-ton steam engine barreling down on you.

Well, at least that confirms I'm on the Iron Beam. I'm pretty sure that was Taylor Siding. So, if I remember right, I should hit – bad choice of words – I should fly over Benyon, Rosebud, Redland, Rockyford, Baintree, Nightingale, Ardenode and Layalta, and by then I should be able to see the bright flares at the Turner Valley oil field.

> *He collects himself and flies on silently.*

(seriously) I think this is the worst, flying at night. Two hundred and fifty advanced flying hours to my name, and still I hate it. It's so hard to see. So damned dark you have to pull your eyes inside out. *(he blinks his eyes hard and shakes his head slightly)* You end up concentrating so hard just trying to see – sometimes it's like trying to see the dry space between falling raindrops.

> *The lights fade out as the Harvard flies off.*

SCENE 16

No.3 S.F.T.S. Calgary – Wings Parade Graduation. There is a military brass band fanfare playing tunes such as the "Air force March" and "The Maple Leaf Forever". The Group Captain enters followed by guests Shirley and Betty. The graduating LACs perform a march-past in formation.

CORPORAL VOICE: Wings Parade, attention!

The LACs come to attention silently. One by one each LAC steps forward and the Group Captain pins his wings on his chest. They exchange salutes and the LAC returns to formation. Gus enters, in his officer's cap, joining Shirley and Betty.

GROUP CAPTAIN: R.U. 27433, Leading Air Craftsman James Edgerton Grady – Commissioned.

Jimmy enters, marches forward to attention and salutes.

(returning the salute) Special Distinction. In recognition of your achieving the highest grades of this December, 1942 graduating class, the officers of No.3 Service Flying Training School, No.4 Training Command, Calgary, hereby present you with this engraved gold wrist chain to take with you to meet the enemy in the skies of war!

The Group Captain presents Jimmy with the wrist chain and an officer's cap and pins his wings on his chest. Jimmy accepts, salutes, and returns to formation. The guests applaud.

CORPORAL VOICE: Wings Parade, dismissed!

The LACs shout "Hurray", toss their caps and congratulate one another. The Group Captain exits and Shirley, Betty and Gus go to Jimmy.

SHIRLEY: *(hugging Jimmy)* Oh, my baby! Oh, and you're an officer! I'm so proud of you, James! *(she removes Jimmy's side cap and he puts his officer's cap on)*

JIMMY: Thanks, Mom.

SHIRLEY: *(kissing him on the cheek)* My little Jimmsy! *(she pulls out her hanky, dabs her tongue with it and then wipes the lipstick from Jimmy's cheek)*

JIMMY: *(embarrassed)* Mom!

GUS: *(grabbing Jimmy's hand)* Bully for you, Balzac!

JIMMY: Rusky, you made it!

GUS: Wouldn't miss it for the world. Congratulations!

JIMMY: *(seeing Gus's officer cap)* Officer Rusky!

GUS: Officer Balzac!

BETTY: *(hugging and kissing Jimmy)* Congratulations, Jimmy!

SHIRLEY: *(confused)* What does he mean calling you "Balzac?" We're from Calgary, Angus, not Balzac! You know that! *(she grabs Jimmy's arm)* James, show me your wrist. Oh, my, it's real gold!

JIMMY: *(looking around)* Mom, did they let Dad come?

SHIRLEY: No dear, I'm sorry. I'm afraid your father wasn't having a good day, so the hospital thought it best to keep him in. You know he wishes you all the best. *(to Gus)* My, and look at you, Angus! The two of you boys, all graduated!

GUS: With "above average" rating, if I do say so myself. We're genuine flyboys now!

A formation of a/c fly low overhead.

SHIRLEY: *(grabbing her hat in preparation for a dousing)* Oh! Not here, too!

JIMMY: What's wrong, Mom?

SHIRLEY: Oh, uh, nothing... it's just the wind surprised me, I guess.

GUS: *(grabbing for Jimmy's wrist)* Let's see that piece of gold... *(he whistles)* Look at that!

SHIRLEY: Everyone, now, together and smile.

Shirley herds the four into a line abreast and a camera flash captures their pose. Jimmy gives the wrist chain to Shirley.

BETTY: I knew you could do it! Once you settled down and concentrated!

Shirley and Betty examine the wrist chain.

GUS: Yeah, speaking of concentrating... *(he pulls Jimmy aside and tosses him a hotel key)*

JIMMY: *(catching the key)* What's this?

GUS: I got us two rooms at the Palliser. One for me and... I forget her name, and one for you and Bets. Let's go!

JIMMY: What? No. No, not the Palliser. Anywhere but there.

GUS: Why the heck not? What's wrong with the ol' Paralyzer? It's a classy enough joint. Besides, who's going to notice the décor anyway? And I guarantee neither of us is going to have time to think about room service!

Jimmy moves himself and Gus a little further out of earshot of Shirley and Betty.

JIMMY: Look, it's not the hotel, okay. It's that First Street and Ninth Ave. Every time I go anywhere near there, there's a damn R.C.A.F. funeral procession. It's the worst thing you can see, Gus, honest – and there's so many of them, all the time, practically. *(he gets more unnerved)* And it seems every single time I'm there on Ninth, right beside the Palliser, and sure enough, all the traffic stops dead, and suddenly you see the whole creepy bunch of them, clumping south along First Street, right past me and the Palliser, right down under the railway underpass, like they're disappearing right down into the depths of hell. I just can't take it, okay? It gets me all cold and shaky, and all I can think is maybe that's what it'll be like when it's my turn.

GUS: Hey, okay, easy now, Jimmsy. It's okay, we can go somewhere else.

JIMMY: I won't go near that place. I heard some Acey-Deucy from Medicine Hat or somewhere bought it last night in a Moth – him and the instructor. And I don't want to be anywhere near anyone's procession on the day I'm graduating.

GUS: Okay, look – I know a guy, maybe he can get us into the National. Okay? Okay?

JIMMY: I don't care, just not the Palliser.

GUS: Okay, it's a done deal. Look, it'll take me a phone call or two, so let's just hit the hangar ballroom first. You relax, take Betty for a spin or two, and I'll come and get you when I've got the National sorted out. Okay?

JIMMY: *(half-heartedly)* Yes, okay, okay. Thanks, Gus.

Gus brings Jimmy back to the women.

GUS: *(to Betty)* Slight change of flight plan. I'll meet you two at the ball in about an hour, tops.

Gus winks at Betty and exits.

BETTY: Oh, alright. *(to Shirley)* Mrs. Grady, there's a big dance in the hangar, would you like to join us for a drink?

SHIRLEY: Oh. Thanks, Elizabeth, but no. You young people go on and do all your celebrating. I have to be getting across town to make my visit to the veterans hospital. *(she grabs Jimmy and kisses him and returns his wrist chain)* I am just so proud of you, James! And so is your father! *(to Betty)* You take good care of my boy, Betty.

BETTY: I will, Mrs. G.

Shirley kisses Betty on the cheek and then exits. The scene and lighting transforms the area into a gala graduation dance floor inside the hangar, replete with revolving crystal ball and a big band playing a medley of tunes such as "Don't Sit Under the Apple Tree", "I'll Never Smile Again" and "Moonlight Becomes You". The graduated airmen dance with R.C.A.F. W.D.s, civilian girls and even relatives.

Betty and Jimmy begin to dance, but he pulls her off to a quiet corner downstage.

BETTY: *(cuddling into Jimmy)* What was that all about with Gus?

JIMMY: Gus is going to find us some accommodations.

BETTY: What do you mean? I've got my Pop's house and you've got...

JIMMY: Not us, silly. Us!

BETTY: *(embarrassed)* Oh, Us!

They kiss and remain holding each other.

JIMMY: You know, the kind with a threshold...

BETTY: *(disappointed)* Oh, you mean getting married.

JIMMY: Only if you want to.

BETTY: Do you want to?

JIMMY: Yeah. I mean, I don't know. That's what half the guys in the Class of '42 are doing, except maybe Gus.

BETTY: Yeah.

JIMMY: I bet he was giving special tutoring to the guys on the train all the way down from Edmonton! *(they laugh)* But if you want to wait, Bets, that's okay. I mean, if you're not ready...

BETTY: It's not that, Jimmy. I am ready. I've been ready for ages! It's just...

JIMMY: What?

BETTY: I'm scared, I guess.

JIMMY: Well, I don't exactly know the flight plan, either.

BETTY: No – I mean, I'm scared that, if we do get married, make it official, before you leave...

JIMMY: You're not going to jinx me, honest!

BETTY: I know that. It's just... I have this terrible feeling that, if we do go ahead and marry now, then you'll always have that weighing on the back of your mind. I don't mean you'd be thinking of it on purpose, but in your subconscious, it'll always be there. You'll be a married pilot, with responsibilities, and no matter how much you try not to let it affect you, it will. It will be a distraction, which isn't a problem on the ground, but when you're at twenty-thousand feet, it could be just enough to niggle away at you, and suddenly you're not as spontaneous as you should be, or maybe it'll pop into your head right when you need to make a right decision... I don't want our marriage to make you responsible to me, to anyone. Because as soon as that happens, it could be the one moment when you second-guess yourself, because of me, and that moment when you're not completely committed to an action you have to take... it could kill you, Jimmy.

JIMMY: *(holding her)* Shhhh...

BETTY: Call it fate, or voodoo or plain old Aurora Borealis – I know it's silly, but, maybe in peacetime, when we're just bush flying, it wouldn't be such a distraction. How can we risk it when you're going off to war?

JIMMY: Sooo, let me get this straight. You're okay with us sleeping together as much as we want, you just don't want to tie the knot?

BETTY: Do you mind?

JIMMY: Uh, I think I can manage that. But as soon as I come back, I want us to get married, and I want to go up north. We can both fly for your Dad's old company 'til we save enough to start up our own air service.

BETTY: Oh, yes, Jimmy!

JIMMY: So I guess I'll just have to wait for you.

BETTY: I'll wait for you.

JIMMY: I mean it. I'm not Gus. I will wait.

BETTY: I know.

> *They embrace and kiss.*

Promise me you'll take care of yourself – Gus, too, if you can... I love you.

JIMMY: I love you. Now what do you say we get busy with some pre-marital practice?

BETTY: Oh, yes! Let's!

JIMMY: We've got to meet Gus and his latest girl at the National.

> *Gus hurries in, with two new hotel room keys.*

GUS: Okay, here we go – a one-afternoon trip to the grand old National Hotel. *(he hands one key to Jimmy)*

JIMMY: *(giving Betty the key)* Here's the room key. You go on ahead. Me and Gus will find some liquor.

> *Jimmy kisses Betty and she exits.*

GUS: There's just one small problem.

JIMMY: What?

GUS: The last minute hotel swap cost us. How much cash do you have?

JIMMY: I gave you everything I had.

A group of new recruits in their sweatsuits enter.

GUS: What's this?

JIMMY: I heard there's a logjam at the Manning Depot. Too many joining up. So they're warehousing recruits anywhere they can 'til space becomes available.

GUS: Well, well. Our prayers are answered. Follow my lead. *(shouting orders)* Recruits, attention! Form up!

The recruits form up, facing upstage.

Look at you! Corporal Prune, these have got to be the sorriest bunch of recruits the R.C.A.F. has ever seen!

JIMMY: That they are, sir.

GUS: Alright, Corporal Prune prepare the men for inoculation! Collect the five dollar fee from each man. Come on. Come on.

JIMMY: Yes, sir! *(shouting)* Recruits! Present funds!

The recruits reluctantly surrender their money.

GUS: You don't expect the air force to pay for everything, do you?

JIMMY: Recruits! About face!

The recruits turn to face downstage.

(shouting) Prepare for inoculation! Bend over! And, drop your drawers! Now, lower your shorts and show us some flesh!

GUS: Now you will remain in this position until you receive your inoculations. Understood?

*Remaining bent over with their trousers down and their
undershorts half-lowered exposing their upper buttocks, the
recruits awkwardly hold their trousers up with their left hands
and try to salute with right hands.*

RECRUITS: *(facing the floor)* Yes, sir!

> *Gus and Jimmy run off when they see the Corporal entering.*

CORPORAL: What the…? Why is it every time I get a new batch of
knuckleheads, the first thing I have to see on them is their lily-white
arses? *(shouts)* Now pull up your pants and get back to marching on
the common! *(grumbling)* And they're aiming to train thirty-thousand
of these dopes in '43!

> *The recruits comply and the Corporal herds them off. Music such
> as "In the Mood" comes up.*

Blackout

END OF ACT 1

ACT TWO

A C.P.R. train whistle blows long and mournfully. On top of the whistle, a ship's horn blasts two launching toots and fades out. Then the C.P.R. whistle fades into a British train whistle blowing short and abrupt.

SCENE 1

No.3 Pilot Reception Centre, Bournemouth, England. A brass band launches into a rousing rendition of "The Maple Leaf Forever". A large contingent of R.C.A.F. airmen, gathered into parade formation, marches in. Jimmy is one of the leading flag bearers.

DRILL SERGEANT VOICE: *(shouting orders over the music)* Royal Canadian Air Force, Bournemouth. Parade presentation, attention.

The airmen halt and come to attention. An air raid siren begins to wail, growing progressively louder. The airmen remain at attention, but their eyes nervously scan the sky. The band peters out as various musicians stop playing; the airmen hesitate, then finally scatter, leaving Jimmy standing with his flag. An M.E.-109 roars low toward Jimmy and he freezes. Gus runs in carrying two gas mask kits, grabs Jimmy and they huddle in a corner as the M.E.-109 roars over. Its two 13mm machine guns rip up the ground where the ceremony had been. The M.E.-109 and the air raid siren fade out.

JIMMY: Rusky! When did you get here?

GUS: My tug got us here about a week before you.

The All Clear siren sounds briefly.

81

JIMMY: *(huddling again)* Not again?

GUS: *(getting up and dusting himself off)* That's the All Clear. You better get to know the difference between the two, Balzac. There's not a lot of time for practicing over here.

JIMMY: *(gets up)* Piece of cake.

GUS: First order of business. You never go anywhere without one of these.

> *Gus hands one of the gas mask kits to Jimmy.*

JIMMY: A picnic box?

GUS: Yeah. But you don't have to worry about ants because they'll all be dead from gas attack.

JIMMY: The travel brochures never mentioned these – or the higher-ups.

GUS: Just as well. Otherwise half your boat would have walked the gang-plank rather than think about the prospects of gas. *(lightening up)* Just trying to keep you alive, kiddo.

JIMMY: Put it on my tab. Listen, I'm getting a Halifax. Please tell me you're not crewed up yet.

GUS: I'm all yours, Skipper, and I don't mind telling you, it's been mighty interesting, me trying to come up with excuses to avoid other crews and kites. So you'd better appreciate me.

JIMMY: Never doubted you, Rusky.

> *Hillis enters walking backwards, carrying his kit and defending himself from an encounter off-stage.*

JIMMY: *(to Gus)* What's this?

HILLIS: Cripes, ease it up, Sheilagh! Cripes, Kate!

GUS: *(shaking his head)* More moves than a chicken full of Exlax. *(to Hillis)* Hey, Hops – keep that up and you won't live long enough for the Luftwaffe to get a good shot at you!

HILLIS: *(turning to Gus and Jimmy, then coming to attention and saluting)* Cracky! I thought Canada was bad enough when it came to wooing the girlies. Sir.

> *Jimmy and Gus return the salute.*

GUS: Everything is rationed here, mate!

JIMMY: *(indicating Gus)* And believe me, he should know. You got a crew yet?

HILLIS: No, sir. *(offering his hand)* Sergeant master Bomb Aimer/ Forward Gunner extraordinaire Harold K. Hillis, Royal Australian Air Force.

JIMMY: *(shaking his hand)* Then welcome aboard. R.C.A.F. Pilot Officer James Grady. This is Rusky... I mean, R.C.A.F. Flying Officer Angus Minton, Navigator.

HILLIS: *(eyeing Gus)* Russian?

GUS: It's a long story, Hops. But no, I'm Canadian to the quick.

> *R.A.F. Mid-Upper Gunner Darby and R.C.A.F. Rear Gunner Frenchy enter and salute Jimmy and Gus.*

JIMMY: Guns!

GUS: Crewing up is weird. Kind of reminds me of my first date.

JIMMY: *(to Gus)* It's called dumb luck.

GUS: *(to the two gunners)* Are you crewed up yet?

DARBY: No, sir.

GUS: Good. You are now. *(as he does the introductions, everyone shakes hands)* R.C.A.F. Flying Officer Angus Minton Navigator. Your skipper is R.C.A.F. Pilot Officer James Grady, and this is R.A.A.F. Sergeant Bomb Aimer/Air Gunner Hops Hillis.

DARBY: R.A.F. Sergeant Mid-Upper Air Gunner Quinton Darby.

FRENCHY: R.C.A.F. Sergeant Tail Gunner Louis Brébuf, No.9 Bombing and Gunnery, Mont Joli, Québec.

GUS: Well, a French-trained flyboy!

FRENCHY: Yes, sir, but I got my lessons in English, just like everybody else.

JIMMY: *(to Frenchy)* But are you any good?

FRENCHY: Sir, the first day we got to shoot, they put us in a line side-by-each and every man had five rounds to shoot at his own target. The guy beside me missed his target with every shot. But when the instructor looked at my target there were ten holes. That's when I knew I was a great gunner.

GUS: Well, that's good enough for me. So, here we are. The makings of Balzac's Best!

JIMMY: We still need a Flight Engineer and a Wireless.

> *A veteran R.A.F. Flying Officer Flight Engineer approaches. He is deep in thought.*

> *(to the F/E)* Hey, bud! Do you know where we can get a good Flight Engineer?

> *The F/E keeps walking past.*

GUS: Hey, England! My skipper asked you if you know any good Flight Engineers.

FLIGHT ENGINEER: *(he stops, lights a cigarette, exhales slowly)* Yeah.

GUS: Well? Where can we get a hold of them?

FLIGHT ENGINEER: Try France – you'll find them all in little bloody pieces somewhere between here and France. *(he starts to walk away)*

JIMMY: *(calling after him)* Well, how about you? Have you got a kite? What's your name and where are you from?

FLIGHT ENGINEER: *(he stops, with his back to the group)* Sir, if you don't know my name, you won't have it to forget. *(he walks away)*

JIMMY: What the hell was that all about?

GUS: Never mind. We don't need a gloomy cuss jinxing the whole crew. Come on, we'll find somebody over at the mess. Oh, and I want to run over to Bobby's Department Store, before it closes.

JIMMY: What for?

GUS: I want to invest in a flashlight, I mean, a torch, to shine my way to the girlies during the blackouts.

The group of five exit.

SCENE 2

Gus and Jimmy are near the entrance to their barracks. Gus is on the ground, collecting his dice and the money he has won from a game of craps. Jimmy warily scans the foggy sunset sky.

JIMMY: Hell's bells! You know, on the prairies, when that wind blows in from the mountains, it's like the weather just gallops on in, all excited and fired up, like it's in a real big hurry, like it's just got to gallop through Alberta to see the rest of the country real quick. Visibility 25 miles at 3,000 feet A.G.L.! You get caught up in that and it makes you want to hop in a kite and chase the wind clear across to the Great

Lakes and back! When you were too excited to sleep, the Instructor would always say "Relax, kiddo! The sky will be there tomorrow!" And you know, he was right.

GUS: *(he cleans off and kisses his dice and carefully pockets them)* Uh-huh. *(he counts the money he's won)*

JIMMY: You know what I miss most? The Chinook. I remember it was always like… like a slate-gray sheet of cloud tucked up tight under the chin of the prairie sky, with just enough room for its brilliant blue head to peak past the flannel and give a sunlit wink to Ol' Man Winter below.

GUS: *(he pauses counting and remembers the Canadian prairies)* 'Cept one little spark from a steer's behind, and that wind can spread a fire storm straight across the prairie.

JIMMY: Yeah, I guess. *(pulling up his collar)* But here – it's so foggy the frigging birds are walking. Here, the stuff oozes in and drops, all wet and sour, like the sea is backed up and spilling over, and it's got no reason to move. Like it's going to spew on everything. It gets in everywhere, and it can swallow a Halifax whole, worse than black ice can eat up a truck. Two to five miles, tops, at fifteen hundred feet, above sea level, if you're lucky. Here, you just can't be sure the sky is going to be there again tomorrow.

They're both quiet, with twinges of homesickness.

GUS: *(shaking himself out of his thoughts and rising)* Cut the line-shoot, Shakespeare! There's a "war on tonight!"

JIMMY: *(hesitating)* Gus, do you ever get scared?

GUS: It's scary. Sure, I'm scared. But I'm not afraid. Everybody owns their own fear – and I try to keep mine from slopping over onto anyone else.

JIMMY: *(quietly)* I heard an R.A.F. crew telling some new boys the average life expectancy in Bomber Command is six weeks.

GUS: Yeah? Well, the average life span of a craps game with loaded dice is a lot shorter, so that should keep us on our toes. *(he gets up)* Let's get over to Briefing before we miss it altogether.

They both move straight into the next scene.

SCENE 3

> *Gus and Jimmy switch to their battle dress jackets and join other crews in the smoke-filled Briefing Room. The sounds of several crews crowded into the room are heard. The rest of their crew, including Sergeant F/E Fred "Skinner" Langdon and R.C.A.F. Sergeant WOp Francis "Fever" Felverton join them. All sit on benches downstage, facing the audience. A blood-red curtain is projected onto their faces.*

COMMANDER VOICE: Gentlemen, it's not exactly the Happy Valley, but the Target For Tonight is...

> *A map of the French coast, with a reconnaissance photo on the side, is projected onto the faces of the crews. Routes of thin red lines, flak areas of red circles, and searchlights as blue circles, are marked all over the map. The shadow of the Commander's pointer stick points to routes and elements as he mentions them.*

...the Krupp Iron Works at Essen.

> *The crews mumble their approval and excitement. Throughout the briefing Jimmy and Gus study their maps and photos, making notes and taking measurements.*

You will be joining over a thousand other kites. I don't need to remind you, that's well over six thousand aircrew.

> *Again, there are mumbles of excitement.*

As you can see from your Target Map, you will hit the main factory buildings here, here, and here. If you can leave a mark on the main Berlin rail line here, or any one of these others here, so much the better. Your best approach will be from here, and then straight up the Ruhr.

You will note heavy flak areas here, here, and here. You should adjust your course randomly to avoid flak bursts safely. Thanks to the last thousand kite show on Cologne, the searchlights here, and here should still be out of commission, but you'll want to keep a sharp eye out, all the same. As for night fighters – well, it should be pretty quiet out there.

Remember, don't risk aircraft unnecessarily. As soon as you form up, keep watching all around you. Your objective is to go in, bomb your target and return safely. Any questions?

The crews are quiet.

And whatever you do, don't forget the Colours of the Day! Wireless Ops, you can pick up your call signs directly from me. Right. Have a good show, give them a good thumping, and good luck. Now, let's hear from the Met. Man.

GUS: Windy!

As the Met. Man goes through his briefing, the crew members turn to one another and mouth his first and last phrases.

MET. MAN VOICE: The weather should be fine.

CREW MOUTHING: The weather should be fine.

MET. MAN VOICE: Moderate cumulus cloud, ceiling at 2,500 feet; navigational winds northwest – 30 miles per hour at all heights; visibility 10 miles…

MET. MAN VOICE: Risk of fog at dawn.

CREW MOUTHING: Risk of fog at dawn.

MET. MAN VOICE: Good luck, chaps.

COMMANDER VOICE: Keep your bottoms down, your heads up, and give 'em hell! Strike hard! Strike sure!

Jimmy and his crew gather at their lockers in the cramped crew room, donning their gear, Mae Wests, equipment, flasks of tea or soup, etc. in preparation for the night sortie. Frenchy, who has the coldest position, puts on several layers of clothing under his flying suit. They do everything in a very practised and almost ritualistic manner; everything goes on in exactly the same way, in exactly the same order, as before every sortie.

FEVER: *(with his kit)* Skipper, I've got everything, so I'm going over to get my colours.

JIMMY: Okay, Fever. Make it lickety-split.

Fever exits.

SKINNER: Jeeze, Frenchy, you look godawful!

FRENCHY: Lie off, plow boy.

GUS: *(to Jimmy)* What's up with him?

JIMMY: Go easy. He's sick because he had to sit backwards on the train all the way up from London this morning.

GUS: So?

JIMMY: So, when he has to sit backwards he gets sick.

SKINNER: Frenchy, you're a tail gunner, for crying out loud! You sit facing the wrong way from here to Goring's house and back! How come you can't sit backwards on a train?

FRENCHY: When I'm up in the kite, I've got my .303s and twenty-four hundred rounds ready to shoot, and all I need to see is bandits coming at me, so I don't have to see the world tumbling backwards, you know? Ah, never mind. I guess you have to come from the backward town like Lac St. Jean to understand.

GUS: What you need is some *Kwells* pills. Those will keep your chuck from upping!

FRENCHY: *(he pats his inner pocket)* I just stocked up, sir.

HILLIS: *(to Gus)* Don't worry, sir. Our rear mate here is just a bit dumbfounded – which is to say, when he was found, he was dumb!

SKINNER: You're the one from down under, wise guy.

GUS: Just you don't get so mixed up back there you sit facing the wrong way and start firing up my keester! I heard those Yanks in their B-17s have twenty-seven feet of ammunition in each of their guns, and they swear they're not happy unless they've used the whole nine yards on every raid.

DARBY: *(to Frenchy)* Just remember to fire the right way. It's me who's next in line up that Hali's gut!

HILLIS: *(to Darby)* Buckshee for you, mate!

The crew bus is heard driving up, stopping and honking its horn.

JIMMY: Let's shake a leg everyone.

GUS: Lickety-split, Skip.

The crew moves straight into the next scene.

SCENE 4

Jimmy and his crew, joined by Fever, arrive at the Halifax. For a moment, each man freezes in a rough lineup, silhouetted in darkness, in front of their a/c, in a classic 7-man "crew before battle" pose. They break out of this pose, the silhouette light effect goes down and they mill around: Darby throws his ammunition boxes aboard the forward area and then smokes a cigarette, Gus double-checks his Nav sack, Fever double checks his Signals sack and his Colours of the Day, Hillis flips through his portfolio of bombing maps and photos, Skinner pulls off his flying boot to remove a stone, and Frenchy hauls his boxes of ammunition aboard the aft area.

JIMMY: Chinook all the way, fellas.

FRENCHY: What?

GUS: It's a wind called a Chinook. It's only in Alberta. It's good. The Indians call it a Snoweater, because in the winter the temperature can go from minus ten to plus twenty in an hour, and it's so warm it can melt inches of snow in a single day.

HILLIS: *(he mimics his story)* Oh, I remember those right enough, out in the west of your Canada, sir. I trained in Lethbridge, so I know about Alberta wind. Let me explain it to you, Frenchy, mate. It's like Mother Nature eats her belly full of too many of those prairie oysters…

DARBY: What in god's name is a prairie oyster?

FRENCHY: Seafood on the prairies? He's full of it!

GUS: It's the balls off a calf.

FRENCHY: What?

DARBY: Gaw, you Canadians. And you turn your noses up at kidney for supper!

GUS: They're a delicacy. Just fry them up in a little butter.

FRENCHY: Excuse me, sir, but I say all you plow boys are crazy.

HILLIS: *(acting out his words)* Anyway, so somewhere up in the Rocky Mountains, Mother Nature eats herself a belly too full of those slippery delicacies. So she turns to face the Pacific, her arse to the east, hikes up her skirts, bends over, and let's rip with the God-almightiest biggest fart, and all this lovely warm air comes rushing west, straight into Alberta!

FRENCHY: I'll stick with the cold in the east, thanks.

HILLIS: Truth told! In fact, the fart is so strong, it forms this big, dis-stink-tive mass of clouds that look like they've all been stopped dead in one straight line in the western sky.

GUS: The wind is so strong, it can make for inverted landings – but it makes for a nice warm break in the middle of winter.

JIMMY: *(he hands his wrist chain to Gus)* Hang on to this for me, will you, Rusky?

GUS: *(taking the chain)* You got it, Balzac.

> *The crew board their Halifax bomber, single file, through the side hatch in the aft section via a spindly metal ladder or by hoisting themselves up. The fuselage is extremely cramped. The men can touch each side with their outstretched arms, and all must walk crouched over to keep from hitting their heads. Frenchy is first in and turns to the tail. The rest enter in order of the closest to the forward positions and back: Hillis in the nose, Gus behind him to the curtained navigation table under the cockpit, then Jimmy at the controls. Only the pilot actually wears his parachute, sitting on it like a cushion. The rest of the crew members stash their chutes nearby or on hooks, and Frenchy's chute is the furthest away of all.*

SKINNER: *(as he enters aft toward his flight engineer position facing port side, he hits his shin on the main spar)* Shit!

> *Fever follows to his wireless operator position behind Skinner,*

92

and Darby is last, ditching his cigarette and then going to his mid-upper gunner position. Each man plugs in his leather flying helmet/oxygen mask intercom and must activate the microphone by hand each and every time he speaks into it. If unplugged, he can shout above the noise of the engines.

JIMMY: *(on intercom)* Check, check. Report in.

GUS: Check.

HILLIS: Check.

SKINNER: Check.

DARBY: Check, Skipper.

FEVER: Check.

FRENCHY: Check.

> *Everyone does his pre-flight check at his station. Gus lays out his maps and instruments, Fever tunes the wireless, Hillis sets his bomb aimer scope and checks the forward gun, Darby and Frenchy check their respective guns and ammunition, and Jimmy and Skinner begin their flight checks.*

JIMMY: *(checking each control and gauge)* Oil Gauge: okay.

SKINNER: Master Fuel Gauge: okay.

JIMMY: Fuel Tank Selectors: okay.

SKINNER: Booster Pump Switch: okay.

JIMMY: Fuel Pressure Warning Lights: off.

SKINNER: Emergency Air Control Switch: off.

JIMMY: Emergency Oil Dilution Switch: off.

SKINNER: Fuel Booster Pumps: ammeter checks okay.

JIMMY: Starboard Inner Ground/Flight switch: on ground. Throttles: set. Pitch: fully fine.

SKINNER: Slow Running: Idle cut off.

JIMMY: Supercharger: M Gear - lights out. Air Intake: cold. Rad Shutters: auto. No.2 Tank: selected, booster pump on. Master Fuel: on. Ignition: on. *(he checks out the port window)* Contact! Clear!

SKINNER: *(he checks out the starboard window)* Clear!

> *The starboard inner engine whines and sputters to life. Frenchy, Darby and Hillis all test the movement of their guns. The starboard outer, port inner, and port outer engines come to life in sequence.*
>
> *The engines are briefly opened up full until the required oil pressure is achieved. The sound is deafening.*

JIMMY: *(talking over the engine noise)* Pressure: okay.

SKINNER: Temperature: okay.

JIMMY: Hydraulics: flaps down, up and indicating.

SKINNER: Bomb Doors: closed.

JIMMY: Booster Pumps: off.

SKINNER: Rad Shutters: open. Magnetos: checked and serviceable.

JIMMY: Ground/Flight Switch: on. Flight Nav. Lights: on. Altimeter: Q.F.E. is set.

SKINNER: Instruments: all serviceable. Suction: four and a half. Rad.

JIMMY: Shutters: open. Brakes: pressures okay.

SKINNER: Chocks Away!

FEVER: *(relays the Tower message)* "J" Jig, stand by to taxi.

JIMMY: "J" Jig, clear to line up. *(resuming the pre-flight checks)* Autopilot: clutch in, switch out. D.R. Compass: set and operating. Pitot heater: on. Trimmer: elevator two forward, others to neutral.

SKINNER: Fuel: contents checked, master switches on, No.2 tanks selected, cross-feeds off, booster pumps on. Superchargers: M Gear. Air Intake: cold. Rad. Shutters: auto. Flaps: set to take-off and indicating.

FEVER: *(to the tower)* Hello Flare-path, hello Flare-path, "J" Jig ready for take-off... *(relays Tower message)* "J" Jig, stand by, temporary delay. Stand by – temporary delay. "J" Jig, shut down and stand by...

The crew groans. Jimmy and Skinner shut down the Halifax and everybody begins to disengage and make their way back out of the a/c and onto the ground. Frenchy, sweating and gasping from heat, is the last to emerge, shoving his considerable gear out and peeling off his extra layers of clothing.

The NAAFI truck is heard screeching up to a stop and honks its horn.

GUS: NAAFI truck. Tea up, boys!

DARBY: Hot tea and a wad!

JIMMY: Oh, no. If I have to sit down to one more sewer trout I might just trade sides.

DARBY: But sir! The King himself loves his sardines on toast. You just haven't had 'em served right, mashed up with a fork and smeared on the toast, bones and all. Oh, I could go for a plate right now!

FEVER: Forget the fish. I'll be glad if I never see another brussels sprout as long as I live. Brussels sprouts boiled, brussels sprouts baked, brussels sprouts creamed...

GUS: Here you go, Balzac.

Gus tosses the wrist chain and Jimmy catches it.

(to Frenchy) Jeeze, Frenchy. One of these days you're going to sweat yourself right into a puddle.

FRENCHY: I'd like to dress one of those tower guys up like a tail gunner at twenty thousand feet and see how long he lasts down here.

Three live rounds fall out of Frenchy's gear: a German 20mm canon round, a U.S. .50 calibre round and a .303 British round.

HILLIS: *(picking up the rounds)* Here, what's all this, mate? We've never seen these before.

GUS: The bullets are supposed to go in the guns, Frenchy, not in your pockets.

FRENCHY: I carry them to remind me of how good I have to be. *(he grabs the rounds back from Hillis, holds up the 20mm round)* Look, this is a 20mm round. That's what a Messerschmitt 109 is firing out of his nose canons. *(holds up the .50 round next to the 20mm)* This is a .50 calibre round. That's what all the Yanks fire from their Flying Fortress guns. *(holds up the .303)* And this, mes frères, is a British .303 bullet and this is what I fire from my tail guns – same as the infantry use in their rifles.

All are silent.

And believe it or not I have scored two partial kills on German fighters on our tail. Any more questions? Because I'll go up right now with any of you for a little demonstration. *(to Hillis)* How 'bout it, my mate?

DARBY: I'll put a fiver on Frenchy

JIMMY: Alright, everybody settle down. Frenchy, you do us proud. But this kite isn't going anywhere. I've closed my office for the day, thanks.

The light fades and an air raid siren starts to wail. Bombs are heard exploding nearby.

GUS: Right, boys. Let's go and find us some good old Women's Voluntary Service.

Gus races ahead as the rest of the crew follow.

SCENE 5

On 8th Street West in downtown Calgary, fake tear gas begins to waft in. An air raid siren starts to wail and something resembling a trench mortar is heard firing. A Calgary policeman, disguised as a German saboteur, enters, brandishing a homemade Swastika flag.

POLICEMAN/SABOTEUR: *(moving back and forth in the area, he puts on a gas mask and begins yelling through it in a thick Irish brogue)* Heil Hitler! Heil Hitler!

Shirley's friend Grace, already upset, stumbles out of the picture theatre and is alarmed by the situation.

GRACE: Oh dear lord, not Germans! *(she begins whacking the saboteur over the head with her purse)* Help! Police! Get out of here, you! Get out!

POLICEMAN/SABOTEUR: Ow, ow! Stop, lady! Stop!

Shirley hurries out from the theatre, looking for Grace.

SHIRLEY: Grace! Wait! Are you out here? The picture's about to start. Why did you go running out? *(she finally sees Grace hitting the saboteur and shrieks)* Grace!

GRACE: I've had enough. It's too much. We must be six thousand miles from Europe, so however you got here, go back where you came from! *(she grabs at the flag and continues whacking him)*

POLICEMAN/SABOTEUR: *(pulling off his gas-mask)* Jesus, Mary and Joseph! What are you doing? And stop hitting me!

SHIRLEY: *(shrieking and hurrying to Grace)* Grace! No!

GRACE: *(whacking harder and trying to kick at him)* You dirty, stinking, filthy Nazi!

POLICEMAN/SABOTEUR: *(he finally grabs her arms)* I said stop *(angry)* Stop, now! *(he grabs her purse and throws it down)*

SHIRLEY: *(she intercedes and pulls Grace away)* We're sorry, officer. She's just upset, that's all, from the newsreel. She doesn't know what she's doing.

GRACE: Let me go. And you, you stupid Nazi or whatever you are, you leave us alone!

POLICEMAN/SABOTEUR: This is a civil defence exercise, lady.

SHIRLEY: It's true, Gracie. I read about it in the newspaper, how it was going to happen somewhere downtown today. *(to the saboteur)* She didn't mean anything by it, officer.

POLICEMAN/SABOTEUR: I suppose you think the blackout exercises we held last October were an inconvenience, too! For two cents, I'd haul you down to the station. There's a war on! You better be prepared!

SHIRLEY: Yes, of course, officer. We'll just go back into the theatre and let you carry on. Come on, Gracie.

Gracie refuses to budge and instead begins whimpering. The sound of a mortar is heard.

Lordy, what was that?

POLICEMAN/SABOTEUR: It's just fireworks, to sound like mortar fire. Now get out of here, and don't bother any more officers carrying out this important exercise! *(he stomps out)*

SHIRLEY: *(calling after him)* We won't bother anyone. And thank you *(to Grace)* Gracie, what on earth were you thinking?

GRACE: *(weeping)* I can't take it any more. I hate it, I hate it, I hate it.

SHIRLEY: What?

GRACE: The war! It's everywhere – the radio reports, the newspapers, the newsreels, the pictures – nothing but war.

SHIRLEY: I know, but you love James Cagney. Why don't we go back in and watch the picture?

GRACE: *(angry)* Captains of the Clouds! A war picture! And not just the war, but the Canadian air force! It's too much!

SHIRLEY: *(she holds Grace near to her)* I know, dear.

GRACE: Everywhere you look around here, military this and military that. And we're supposed to suddenly hate all Germans. What's the poor Luder family and their nice delicatessen supposed to do now that we're not supposed to buy their goods? What have they ever done to anyone? And the Japs, and the Italians. My husband comes home from work and says we have to hate the Italians too.

SHIRLEY: I don't like it, either, but we are at war with them. Your own Barry joined the air force last summer.

GRACE: I'm sick of it. The newsreels show our leaders posing with our boys, before they ship them off to god only knows what. But they won't be there to greet the coffins coming home, will they? Will they?

SHIRLEY: *(quietly)* Well, no. But I don't think the coffins come home at all. They'll be buried where they fall, I guess.

GRACE: Over there, and we'll never even see their graves

SHIRLEY: *(quietly)* I know.

GRACE: And we're left here on the prairies while they hold stupid air raid drills.

Both women feel spent and fall silent. Shirley, still holding Grace, picks up the purse.

SHIRLEY: *(trying to regain her composure)* Come on, Gracie. Let's get out of this upheaval and get a cup of tea. Hmm?

Grace takes her purse and lets Shirley guide her slowly off.

SCENE 6

It is very dark. The operational light aboard the Halifax brightens slightly. The a/c is cruising at 20,000 feet. The crew members are heard either via plugging in to the intercom, or shouting over the noise. Fever has crawled back to the rear gun turret.

HILLIS: *(frantic, as something wet splashes his head and arm)* Cripes, Kate! The hydraulics line has ruptured! The hydraulics line has ruptured! Skipper!

JIMMY: Relax. The piss-pipe's frozen, you dope. You don't have to announce it to all of occupied France, for crying out loud.

HILLIS: Oh, well, that's alright. A little piss won't matter. It's my natty uniform I was worried about. Hydraulics fluid leaves a nasty stain, and you know how the girls love my uni!

Electric blue St. Elmo's Fire zaps around Jimmy and throughout the Halifax.

DARBY: Jeeze, Skipper, now that we're through them storm clouds, we're glowing like a four-alarm fire! All bluey white, it is.

SKINNER: *(intrigued)* Hey, Skip, if I pissed into St. Elmo's, would I get electrocuted?

JIMMY: Just keep your eyes peeled. Rusky, have we crossed into Germany yet?

GUS: We must have, because everyone's stopped waving. *(pause)* And you'll have one degree correction for the home trip.

JIMMY: One degree, okay.

FEVER: *(coming back to his position, banging his shin on the main spar – he mouths "Shit!" returns to his seat and plugs in)* Skipper, Frenchy's left hand is just about froze! It's hard to see, but his fingers look like they're blacker than flak!

JIMMY: Can he still handle his guns and his mike?

FEVER: Says he can. *(he loosens his jacket)* He should sit here for a while – he'd be sweating his head off pretty quick. I got his oxygen connector working right, too. I don't think it was working right 'cause he was sounding kind of dopey.

SKINNER: What's different about that?

JIMMY: Everyone, re-check that you know where your chutes are and make sure you can reach them.

FEVER: Check.

DARBY: Check.

GUS: Skip, the ones with parachutes left an hour ago.

JIMMY: Just check it, Rusky.

FRENCHY: Skipper, I can see it behind me but my hands can't feel it.

SKINNER: Check.

JIMMY: Fever, if it looks like we're going to have to punch out, on my order, you will go and assist Frenchy – if we need to.

FEVER: Aye, Skipper.

JIMMY: And Rusky?

GUS: Balzac?

JIMMY: If we hit the silks and you see me pass you on the way down, assume command.

GUS: Oh, I'll assume, alright.

Bursts of flak begin flashing all around, causing audible "whumpf" sounds as they explode, followed by rattling sounds as the metal shrapnel hits the Halifax.

FEVER: Jeeze, there's so much flak you could light a cigarette just by holding it out the window.

JIMMY: Rusky, E.T.O.T.?

FEVER: *(watching off starboard)* Jeeze! "C" Charlie got hit! She's cracked down onto X-ray!

Yellow-orange light from the explosions of the colliding a/c plays through the Halifax perspex.

GUS: Estimated Time Over Target four minutes, Skipper.

A blinding searchlight flashes through and past the fuselage.

JIMMY: Hillis, stand by to toggle your bombs. Throttling back to glide.

HILLIS: Aye, Skip – but all I can see is the light from the flares – there's too much cloud.

GUS: We're right where we're supposed to be, Hops.

JIMMY: Target what you can.

DARBY: They've coned "R" Robert!

> *There is a sudden direct hit on the port inner engine. The fuel line explodes and Jimmy screams as his face and hands are sprayed with burning fuel. He struggles to maintain control as the cold outside air rushes into the cockpit, adding to the din of the remaining engines.*

SKINNER: *(shouting)* Skipper! *(on radio)* Skipper's hit! *(he reaches to grab the yoke)*

JIMMY: *(shouting)* Leave it, leave it! We're on target!

> *Fever grabs a pump fire extinguisher and puts out the fire. There is another close flak burst.*

DARBY: She's going down! I think it's "R" Robert!

SKINNER: *(back at his F/E position)* Feathering the port inner now.

GUS: *(poking his head out from behind his curtain)* Forget the damn target, Jimmy! Let Skinner take it and let's get out of here!

JIMMY: What the hell do you want us to do? Turn an orbit and plow straight into the rest of the stream behind us? We've gotten this far, so we're dropping our load. Fever, get me a shot! Go!

> *Fever scrambles past Darby to retrieve the first aid kit.*

Hops, make your run!

HILLIS: Aye, Skip. Bomb doors open. Okay steady, steady, right.

JIMMY: *(shouting)* Skinner, help me with the controls.

SKINNER: *(he scrambles back to help Jimmy)* Aye, Skip.

HILLIS: Right, left a little – steady, steady – slow, right slightly – steady... *(he toggles the bomb switch and the bombs drop)* Bombs gone! Bomb doors closed... Wait, something's off...

Going back, Fever checks the bomb bay flare hatch and plugs in.

FEVER: Bomb doors clos... No, wait! Bomb doors open! Repeat, bomb doors open! The cookie's hung up!

JIMMY: Get rid of it!

Hillis crawls out from his nose position and makes his way back to the bomb bay and plugs in.

FEVER: *(he tries to knock the bomb loose)* All the incendiaries are gone... Jeeze, Skip, it's just hanging here, like a turd stuck to a dog's behind...

JIMMY: Corkscrewing starboard.

The Halifax turns violently down and to starboard and the crew hangs on. Hillis, not plugged in, gestures to Fever to open the bomb bay cover. They do so, then they tinker with the hinge clamps and control wiring on the hung-up bomb, trying not to fall through into the rushing wind.

FEVER: It's still cattywompus! Hurry up! The flak's so thick you could get out and walk on it! We're going to get the flak inside the kite!

HILLIS: I don't know, Skip. Maybe if we nose-down it'll loosen.

GUS: Well we can't exactly dive 18,000 feet and scrape our arse across the ground, now can we?

Fever succeeds in loosening the blockage. Hillis scrambles back to the nose, plugs in and retoggles the bomb switch.

HILLIS: Fever, is that bomb gone...?

FEVER: Gone! Gone!

Fever closes the hatch, readies a syringe of morphine, makes his way back to Jimmy and injects him.

GUS: Bombs gone: the sweetest music this side of heaven.

JIMMY: Skinner, check what sort of fuel we've lost from the port inner. If there's any left, I don't want to lose it.

SKINNER: Right, Skipper. *(at his station, he manages the fuel transference from the tanks to the remaining engines)*

JIMMY: Fever, send the "target bombed" signal.

FEVER: Aye, Skip. *(at his station, he taps out the Morse code signal)*

JIMMY: Get us the hell out of here, Gus!

GUS: You got it, Skip. Heading zero four niner, magnetic, and I'll do a star-shoot.

> *Gradually, the light on the Halifax fades to blackness and the engine roar and all sounds fade out.*

SCENE 7

> *Shirley comes out of her house onto the porch, carrying a basket full of wet sheets. She cranes her neck skyward to check for training a/c overhead, then continues on to the clothesline in the yard.*

SHIRLEY: It wasn't so long ago, all the skies were full of was birds and clouds. It used to be you could stand out here and really hear the quiet.

But that was before the war came – before the aeroplanes came. Now the skies are filled with bright yellow trainers of every description, at all hours of the day and night. They've all got a student pilot and an instructor inside; there's even more inside some of the bigger aircraft. Mostly it's the student pilot who's got control. And you can always tell just by watching them stuttering and dipsy-doodling all over the place, trying to learn to keep the thing smooth and doing what they're supposed to be doing.

Nighttime, too. You'd think if whoever's in charge was smart enough to figure out how to make men fly in the sky, they'd have paid more attention to the birds they were trying to imitate. Most birds don't fly in the dead dark of night. Birds don't much fly in the pouring rain or in icy snowstorms. And most birds don't do their fighting in the air; they do battle on the ground just like all the other wild things. They're smart enough to know the odds are too stacked against them.

Men, on the other hand, especially men at war, they seem to lose hold of their common sense when it comes to flying. They're wanting those boys to fly when it's so dark they can hardly see the controls in front of them, to fly in weather so bad even dogs shouldn't be out in it, and to not only take on the enemy way up there in the middle of nothing, but to defeat him, too.

We were pretty quick to learn to recognize all the different signs – the difference between the innocent little double-wing beginners and that ear-splitting whine of the big advanced trainer, the terrible, gurgling sound an engine makes just before it floods with oil and sputters, the eerie, whooshing crackle when it bursts into flame, the horrible cold silence of an engine that suddenly just cuts out completely – and then counting, just like you do after lightning, waiting, forever, 'til either the thing struggles back to life, or the horrible, muffled crash comes when it dives straight into the ground.

They never ever talk about it, but one time Ed told me, even in the Great War, they called it meeting your shadow. An aeroplane's always got a shadow, even at night, from the moon, or even the stars. And the closer an aeroplane gets to the ground, the bigger its shadow gets. The faster a falling aeroplane drops, the faster it converges on its own ghost image. And the moment when both meet, when both become one, that's the moment of impact, shadow and machine, pilot and death.

If any of them ever admitted to praying before they fly, and most of them never would, that's what they'd pray for: "Please, God, don't let me meet my shadow."

A paperboy's bicycle bell rings and a Calgary Herald newspaper is thrown onto the porch. Shirley freezes, then rushes to it. She drops her basket and grabs the paper. She rifles through the first section until she finds the casualty list and reads it urgently. Once done, she is very relieved, and then catches herself, suddenly aware and ashamed of what she's just done.

I can't help myself. I know it's not right, but I have to do it. As soon as I hear that bicycle bell, my heart stops.

Ed and me, when I was eight months carrying Jimmy, we drove up Didsbury way – something about a horse he wanted to have a look at. That was his favourite line. Still is. Whenever he wants to get out of the house, he always says, "I gotta go see a man about a horse."

We drove around for a couple of hours and mostly just ended up getting lost. We never did find the ranch. But by that time we were getting awful hungry, so we stopped for a bite at the Sunrise Café, on Main Street. Pretty good food, run by a nice little Chinaman and his wife. Ed had a big plate of liver and onions, and I remember I had a hamburger – a real treat, with bright red ketchup. It was pretty good. And we splurged and both had big, thick malted milks, too.

There was a filling station next door, and when we walked back out to our truck, Ed wandered over to have a look at a half-ton or something like that. I don't know, I can't remember exactly what.

And I don't know why, but I went over to peek into a wreck that was there. I never do that sort of thing. Never. I'll never forget it. It was sky-blue, with whitewalls – a Studebaker, I think. The front was all crumpled in pretty good, and the windshield was all gone.

For some strange reason, I went right up to it, and I looked right down where the twisted steering wheel was. The seat upholstery was all torn and stained and there was broken glass splinters everywhere. And down on the floorboard, there was a boy's shoe wedged in between the pedals. There was dried blood all over it, and you just knew by looking at it that it was stuck in there so tight they must have had to leave it there and pull the boy's crushed foot right out of it. He must have been in really bad shape.

I don't try to think of that wreck, that picture of the mess inside. It's not something I want to dwell on by choice. But it flashes into my mind, all the time, for no good reason – and I see that scrunched-up bloody shoe just as clear as if it was now. It's a terrible sight.

But what's worse is, every time I see it like that, in my mind, I don't think about who that poor boy might have been, or what his life might have been like, or what his mother felt when it happened. All's I can think is, "Thank God, it's not my boy's shoe." As if I'm just seeing it today, and all I am is thankful, because it's not my boy's shoe.

A bicycle bell rings and she re-opens the newspaper.

And now, every afternoon, when the paperboy throws the Herald onto the porch, I just have to drop what I'm doing and run to look through it. I look on every page in the first section. Some days they don't print one. Sometimes even for a few days, or even a week, you won't find one.

But then, there it is: "Died In Service."

Today, it's the two hundred and eightieth Official List issued by the R.C.A.F. More than seventeen hundred boys dead or reported missing. And I can't stop myself. I read every name. I just have to. Because that's the only way I can know my boy's alright. Pilots and Navigators and Gunners and Bomb Aimers, I have to read all those *other* boys' names – names I recognize, boys I've watched grow up around here.

When their names appear on that list, I'm relieved. I know I can make it to the next list. Because my boy's name isn't one of them.

What kind of a patriotic mother that makes me, I don't know – I just don't know. But I do know I'll never, ever get the picture of that bloodied shoe out of my mind. And I'll never not be glad to read all those other boys' names.

She tightens the paper in her fist, grabs the basket and runs into the house.

SCENE 8

Darby enters, walking an old bicycle, and meets Gus. Gus takes Darby's casual salute.

DARBY: Hello, sir. Here's that copy of your *Wings Abroad*. *(handing over the newspaper)*

GUS: What? *(taking the newspaper and stuffing it into his pocket)* Oh, yeah. Thanks. What did you think of it?

DARBY: Not exactly Fleet Street material, but a good read all the same. It could do with some more R.A.F. coverage, though. We haven't got anything like that, but then we're not thousands of miles away from home.

GUS: The stories are the easiest part. Their biggest job is trying to keep on top of the casualty lists.

DARBY: Aye. *(pause)* Hey, sir. The Padre's holding a service over at the mess – want to come?

GUS: God? Thanks, but you go ahead. I know all about God.

DARBY: Sir?

GUS: You know how you can hear distant sounds more clearly before a storm, 'cause the air is clearer and more humid?

DARBY: Aye.

GUS: Well, it's kind of like that for me. Only I specifically listen to the thunder – that's God. That's one of the few things my old man ever taught me, when he wasn't giving me the belt. Even in his liquored-up stupor, he said it's different now. The thunder, it's different now, in this Year of Our War, nineteen hundred and forty-three.

DARBY: How do you mean, sir?

GUS: There's more junk in the air – more fuel, more fumes, more death, more blood. He always said thunder lost its innocence in the Great War. It's no longer the bogeyman under the bed at night. Now the thunder is God Almighty, shackling the angels, throwing His arms up in disgust at what man is doing all over again, less than twenty-five years later. So, I don't need to hear anything some Padre's got to say. I know God just by listening to the thunder. And the thunder is very different now.

DARBY: If I may ask, sir, what did your father think of you joining up?

GUS: Who knows. Who cares. He hid inside his bottle for most of that war and then just disappeared shortly after this one started. We haven't seen him since.

DARBY: Sir, do you ever hear of blokes getting scared, up there?

GUS: Sure, it happens.

DARBY: Has it ever happened to you, sir?

GUS: I'm always just thankful for terra firma – more firma than terror. *(seriously)* I've got all kinds of opinions on the subject. It's scary. Sure, I get scared sometimes; everybody does.

DARBY: I can't stop thinking, when I know I've hit a Messerschmitt, and I see him going down without punching out, I always wonder, when I die, will the German I killed open the Pearly Gates for me.

GUS: Beats me, bud. Wait a minute, a Kraut helping a Brit? Nothing doing! Besides, what makes you think you won't be headed south, like the rest of us?

DARBY: You've got me there. *(he pauses)* It's starting to really tear me up, sir. I see so many of our kites get hit and in a blink they're heading straight down. *(almost gasping)* An' I can see 'em all, all seven of the boys inside, trying to crawl upwards to the escape hatches while gravity's dragging them back down, and it just makes me gasp for air just thinking about it – like I'm in the Channel in the freezing water, and all the air is getting sucked right out of my lungs...

GUS: Easy, man, easy.

DARBY: *(getting a bit loud)* I don't want to spend my last seconds in this life trying to crawl along a fuselage plummeting to earth! *(he loses his grip on the bicycle and it falls)*

GUS: *(grabbing the bicycle)* Hey, Sergeant! Get a hold of yourself!

DARBY: *(quiet)* Yes, sir. Sorry, sir. *(he struggles with the images in his mind)*

GUS: You just can't think about that sort of thing. Bite your cheek, or dig your nails into your flesh or something, anything, but don't think about it. Don't think about it.

DARBY: Yes, sir.

GUS: *(he shoves the bicycle at Darby)* Especially when we're up there – you've got six of us in your own kite, depending on you. So you do whatever it is you've got to do to train yourself to keep your mind on keeping us alive. Understood?

DARBY: Yes, sir.

GUS: 'Cause if you can't keep your mind on the task at hand, you'll need to find yourself another crew.

DARBY: I understand. I won't let us down, sir.

GUS: Good. I heard some Wing Commander say once, flying in wartime doesn't make you yellow, but if you're already yellow it'll sure bring it out in you. I don't think you're yellow, Darby. I just think you let your mind wander onto things it shouldn't.

Darby nods. Pause.

Come on, let's get both our minds occupied. Forget the Padre. Let's find ourselves a pub, and you can stand me some pints. Can you do that?

DARBY: I can do that, sir.

GUS: Then what are we wasting time for? Let's go.

They exit together.

SCENE 9

East Grinstead Queen Victoria Hospital. Jimmy enters right. He is fully dressed in his uniform, and the burns to the left side of his face and left hand are still reddened, and his hand is a bit stiff. He puts a cigarette in his mouth, works to retrieve a flip-top lighter from his small belt-pocket, then awkwardly lights a cigarette. On the first inhalation, he coughs and hacks on the smoke, and immediately puts the cigarette out.

JIMMY: *(he spits out the tiny bits of tobacco from the cigarette)* I don't know how Gus does it. I know he says it relaxes him, but he's got to be crazy to smoke these things.

R.C.A.F. Pilot Officer Hannigan in his uniform enters left, carrying his duffle bag full of his kit; he has been told to wait here. The left side of his face is badly disfigured from a severe burn; the skin from his forehead to his neck is unnatural and shiny, and very tight. His mouth is pulled tightly to the left so that he must speak out of the right side only. He has no eyebrows and his burned left ear is shriveled and unnatural. He wears his officer's cap cocked to the left and down on his eyes to try to hide his disfigurement. His left hand and parts of his right hand are also burned, and he tries to keep them hidden in his pockets.

HANNIGAN: *(drops his duffle bag on the floor, punctuating the awkward silence)* They told me to wait here. Hannigan, Liam. Pilot Officer, Winnipeg.

Jimmy turns to face Hannigan, then sees his burns and averts his eyes.

This town's got quite the reputation now. East Grinstead: the town that never stares. East Grim is what we call it – it's always more grim than grin when your face has melted.

Hannigan keeps his eyes on Jimmy but finally realizes Jimmy won't look at him.

(he begins speaking, to himself, to Jimmy, to no one) I guess I was one of the first to lose my eyebrows, if not my nerve, to a spray of liquid fuel fire and shattered perspex. And I was definitely one of the first featureless fortunates the R.C.A.F. kindly shipped off to Ireland – so's my melted face wouldn't affect the morale of those still flying, you understand.

(He mimes casting a fishing line) But I soon developed a keen interest in fishing, oh, and the salmon were pukka.

Religion-rich Ireland. As for any sort of personal religion, well, I'd been raised to believe I was Protestant. A lapsed, definitely non-practicing Protestant, but a Protestant all the same. But when I arrived there in the new Republic of the south, I discovered it just wasn't possible for a Hannigan from Killarney to be anything but Catholic. So I unwittingly became my own Irishism: *(he mimics an Irish accent)* "He went to Ireland a Protestant and was coming home a Catholic."

I was, to say the least, confused. Fortunately though, the war's drained every last drop of faith from my soul, so the confusion isn't really an issue. I mean, how could God permit such relentless suffering and carnage in all corners of this world?

113

Anyway, it turned out this Limerick posting was somewhat less than completely useless, because of course it's the main base for all the Allied flying boats. In fact, it's the first point of land for all trans-Atlantic flights. And I just love watching those big Catalina flying boats land. They come in so graceful, and then they thump down like arse-heavy geese.

I guess eventually I started to get used to the stares and whispers of the few civilians I didn't manage to escape, and I was probably staring right back at them wondering how they could remain neutral in the middle of all hell breaking loose all around them. But what I never could stand was the children. Hoards of them everywhere, grimy, little Irish guttersnipes, as filthy and infested as they are desperately poor – and one little devil in particular, who apparently could find no greater entertainment than to trail everywhere after the resident melted flyer with the hairless face and potato-chip ear. He even talked different than the rest. And I lay awake every night with his vicious tauntings echoing in my patched up head.

When I finally got news of my seven-day pass to London, I was elated. Not that I was looking forward to horrifying a different audience with my presence, but after checking in with Doc Tilley here, I can go visit and stay with an irreligious rogue aunt who's not particular about appearances. And typical R.C.A.F., my release got mislaid and only found at the last minute – so very last minute that I almost missed my flight – *(he mimics an Irish accent)* and sure, that wouldn't have been a good thing in any religion.

(miming his actions throughout) So I grabbed a duff full of personals *(picking up his duffle bag)* – dirty laundry mixed in with the clean stuff, and raced off to the flight line. *(he looks back and forth for his aeroplane)* But the only kite doing a run-up was a decrepit, war-weary Lysander. I mean, I remember us back on the prairies, at Elementary Flight Training, roaring with laughter when we watched these inept old gals drifting backward over the airfield when they flew into a stiff headwind! But a kite's a kite, and I'd take a Kraut Junkers eighty-eight, just so long as it got me back to London.

He makes his way to the aeroplane. The sound of the engine comes up, and he shouts over the noise.

So, the Erk mouthed some unhearable words to me, and I nod like I understand, and I clamber into the aft cockpit. Not the Q.E. on wings, but not bad, and pretty roomy considering. I was starting to look forward to my first date with this old Lizzie.

The engine was up to pressure and we'd be airborne shortly, short take-off and all. But then all of a sudden, the Erk climbs up and shoves something big and moving onto the seat with me. A little boy! And not just *any* little boy, but my nemesis, the filthy little insult-spitting guttersnipe, all short pants and pale bare knees and gangly legs! I try desperately to protest to the Erk, but either he can't understand my Canadian accent, or he just plain ignores me. And then, the little cretin accidentally-on-purpose mistakes my foreign gibberish as some kind of warm welcome and was there anything else I could do for him! And in an instant, he's buckled up safe and sound into my harness, snug as a bug and beaming proudly out the canopy.

I fumed under my breath and shot darts from the corner of my good eye, but it was a waste of rage. The little blighter, quite oblivious to my protests, was now deep in concentration, eyes focused fast forward and lips mouthing words of some kind. This was going to be a long Lizzie hop.

We taxi out, the skipper opens the throttles and we start rumbling down the runway. Suddenly beside me, a tiny pale hand was frantically cutting little patterns in the air. Genuflections! The little stowaway was mouthing prayers and genuflecting! Bad enough I'd been outsmarted by an eight-year-old, but a very Catholic eight-year-old who seemed to know something I didn't.

But then, all of a sudden, just like they say when the fairies are upon you, even aboard a geriatric old Lizzie, then came the magic. Suddenly, he wasn't staring at me. Suddenly, he was seeing beyond my melted face. And just minutes aloft and out of the country that left me a hostage to my own conflicting birthrights, me and this serious wee Catholic begin to talk, shouting to one another over the engine roar. No insults, no avoidance of the remnants of my face. This time, his black crackling eyes bore straight and true into mine. We talk each others' ears off! *(he self-consciously touches his hand to his burned left ear)* His name is Joe, and he is, he tells me, an orphan from way up in Belfast, and he's being shipped off to Dublin for transfer to an unknown foster home.

We talked about any and everything, from North American hockey to James Cagney! – to where and what on earth was Canada anyway. *(he mimes pulling out a sandwich in wax paper)* I reached into my pocket and pulled out a cold, greasy fried egg sandwich and gave him half. Still rabbiting on, he virtually inhaled his portion, and I promptly gave him the rest. He asked did I like blood pudding, and when I said it was awful and Canadians used them for hockey pucks, his utter amazement made me laugh. I was transformed.

Together, wee Joe and I gazed out through the perspex and thrilled at all the shapes and creatures and mysteries in the clouds high above any war. It was as if the fairies themselves were guiding our enchanted flight. I wanted to wrap my arms about this pint-sized chin-wagger and put him in my pocket and protect him from harm and bask in the glowing mischiefs sparking in his eyes.

Too soon, we were on final approach to Dublin – journey's end. We neared the runway and, just like before, he grows quiet and starts praying, eyes fixed and concentrating all of his eight-year-old beliefs. And the moment we touch down, my blessed wee Joe looks straight up at me, sheer joy on his face and eyes flashing and fairly crackling with excitement.

(he mimics the boy's Northern Irish accent) "It worked," he grinned. "We made it! I prayed, and we made it. It worked!" And by the grace of God, the wings of old Lizzie, and the prayers of one wee Joe, make it we did.

(to Jimmy) And then I get back here, to this town, where all of us plastic-skinned guinea pigs are allowed to wear our uniforms during hospitalization, like men. And if kids or anyone looks away, they get told, "Don't stare. Don't look away. Those are the Canadians. You look them square in the eye and you thank them."

> *Jimmy crosses to Hannigan and looks him square in the face. He salutes. Hannigan, slowly raises his burned right hand to return the salute. They remain facing one another.*

GUS: *(calling from off-stage, as he is entering)* That's alright, sugar! But like I was saying, I live in Okotoks, back in Canada. My mansion is called Casa Loma and I own the world's biggest silk stockings factory in the country. All in big, beautiful, downtown Okotoks, the biggest city in all of Canada! I'll tell you all about it – indoor plumbing and ten bedrooms and lots of horses!

> *He enters, walking backwards, carrying a box in his arms and a length of hose coiled around his shoulder.*

(to himself) And lots and lots of bull! *(he stops, still facing off-stage)* Hey, Balzac! Come on, let's hit the road! I just got myself a hot date with that fetching little number at the nurse's station. I can even get her sister for you! They're both off duty in an hour and mine's just dying to hear all about my castle in Okotoks...

> *Gus turns and stares as Jimmy turns to face him. He quietly drops the hose to the floor.*

JIMMY: *(quietly)* Hello, Rusky.

GUS: *(shaken)* Shit, Jimmy.

JIMMY: That bad, huh?

GUS: No. No! I'm just amazed to see you still alive and kicking. I mean, come on, the last time I saw you, well, we all thought you were done for.

JIMMY: This is Pilot Officer Liam Hannigan. And we are in East Grinstead.

GUS: I know that.

JIMMY: The town that doesn't stare.

GUS: *(following Jimmy's insistence)* Right. *(looking straight at Hannigan and offering his hand)* Angus Minton, Navigator. *(he awkwardly jokes, pointing to his Navigator's "O" patch on his uniform)* They're supposed to be switching us to an "N" patch soon, so until they do, I figure my occupation is a good ol' flying arse-hole!

Hannigan finally shakes Gus's hand and then picks up his duffle bag and slowly exits.

(back to Jimmy) Who was he?

JIMMY: Another Canadian flyboy.

Gus grabs and shakes Jimmy's hand, then swats him across the shoulders.

GUS: Are you okay?

JIMMY: Sure. Look, straight from the shoulder, how bad's my face?

GUS: *(serious)* It's nothing. Really, kiddo. Nothing a little *Fitche's Saponified* and a dab of *Brylcream* won't fix. It's actually an improvement on your ugly mug!

JIMMY: It's kind of spooky, how it's a lot like my Dad's, but so different. But now, maybe with the scar tissue, we'll look more alike than we ever have.

GUS: Well, that was twenty-five years ago. And after the Jerries set him and his kite on fire, he planted his face onto the fields of France. You, on the other hand, got back – you got us all back.

JIMMY: *(shakes his head)* Better aeroplanes, bigger burns. Better wars, bigger scars. I figure so long as we keep making new wars, we'll keep getting new horrible wounds, and then we'll keep learning new treatments. So really, I'm doing my bit for the advancement of medicine.

But it's hard for the nurses. I saw one on her first day. The guy she was fussing with had hardly any sort of face left, but, being Canadian, the first thing he said to her would have got himself thrown out of a pub. So she said, "You'll get your ears boxed for talk like that!" And right off he says, "Well, Sweetie, you're going to have to wait 'til the good doctors make me some new ears first."

GUS: *(almost confidentially)* But the burns, they didn't get you inside, did they?

JIMMY: *(quietly)* No. I'm surprised, because when it happened, all I remember doing was gasping for air, like I'd just been thrown into freezing water. *(feigning sophistication)* But I guess I won't be wearing a monocle anytime soon.

GUS: *(playing along)* Oh, I say, old boy! *(breaking)* Hey, wait a minute. What is a monocle, anyway? An old aunt of mine used one sometimes. Is it just a dressed up kind of accessory like a pocket watch and chain? Or is it a real eye glass? Is there a whole generation of folks that only had bad eyesight in one eye? *(he careens around)*

> *They laugh. Pause.*

Shit, it's good to see you!

JIMMY: Yeah. So tell me what's new, how is everyone?

GUS: Okay, well, Frenchy's back. And Darby and Hillis, and everyone, they all send their regards, with a reminder that you owe them all a no-spam dinner for all the turbulent flying you did that night. They were all constipated for a week after that cookie hung up. It's just not the same without you at the controls, you know? Oh, and I owe you a fiver.

JIMMY: What for?

GUS: You beat me to a gong! Chest hardware! Do you have any idea how gals adore medals?

JIMMY: *(laughs)* You never could keep your money in your pocket, could you?

GUS: Yeah, well, I'll have to owe you. I'm skint. Betty's going to go through the roof when you tell her! When do you actually receive the thing? What will it be, a Distinguished Flying Cross?

JIMMY: I don't know if it's a D.F.C. or how any of it works. But don't play it up so much. You know the only reason I got it is because a certain Navigator told one heck of a real good story to the C.O. when we got back. If nobody had been there or seen anything in the first place, nobody would ever have known what I did or didn't do, what all of us did that night.

GUS: Well, if I'm playing it up, you're sure doing a good job of playing it down. Don't sell yourself short.

JIMMY: For every guy getting some piece of hardware, there must be a hundred guys doing unimaginable feats of courage and honour and duty that no one's ever going to know about. Think about it. How many medals are getting earned several times over in every kite going down in flames every night?

GUS: *(he changes the subject)* Oh, here, I almost forgot, this is for you.

JIMMY: What do I need a hose for?

GUS: Oh, that. No, that isn't for you. I brought it to impress another of my many dates, but all I got was a smack across my face.

JIMMY: Why would your date need a hose?

GUS: "Hose" she tells me.

JIMMY: No, Gus!

GUS: If I can get her hose, she'll do anything for me – any thing! So I says I can get her miles of hose if she wants, and tell me what colour, too. And she just jumps through the roof she's so excited! No fooling! So I get her fifty feet from the base groundskeeper. But it turns out she means stockings, and she's sure not in a jumping mood anymore, and she slaps my face halfway into next week! I don't know why girls go gah-gah for them. I prefer it when they just draw a seam line up each leg. Saves me time, if you know what I mean. *(handing over the box)* This is for you.

JIMMY: It's from Mom.

GUS: Came for you back at Pickersgill about two weeks ago. I didn't open it. I was dying to, but I didn't.

JIMMY: Or at least you wrapped it back up pretty good?

GUS: Come on, have at her!

JIMMY: *(tearing open the box)* I'm on it. I'm on it.

GUS: *(reaching past Jimmy) Exports*! And *Sweet Caps*! What the... two cartons! And you don't even smoke! Jeeze Louise, you didn't tell her I'm hooked on the things, did you?

JIMMY: I asked her to send them 'cause they're good to trade...

GUS: Oh, who cares. Hand 'em over. *(he opens a pack and lights one up)* And these are way better than the free ones the Yanks are showing off everywhere. A million free *Camels* a week they're pouring into the U.K. and they all taste like roof tar.

JIMMY: Take it easy, chimney breath. *(rummaging in the box)* Here's a letter! *(he holds up a sheet of paper which has had all but a few words blacked out)* "Dear James... Christmas... twenty-five... Safeway... Love to Gus... Mom and Dad." Well, nothing like news from home. *(he digs in the box and pulls out two rolls of toilet tissue, very excitedly) Purex*!

GUS: Jeeze, forget the cigarettes! That's worth its weight in gold! *(repeating the jingle)* "It's fleecy soft!"

JIMMY: Oh, I get it *(he grabs the letter again)* – they were on sale at Safeway, two rolls for a quarter. *(he quickly stashes the rolls back in the box)* And it'll cost you more than a squirt of gold for a sheet. *(holding up the censored letter again)* As if the Nazis could further their war plans by finding out the price of *Purex* at a prairie Safeway.

(unwrapping the last items) Chocolate and gum, *Smith Brothers* cherry cough drops.

GUS: Come on, let's get out of here. Oh, here – I thought you'd be wanting this back.

Gus gives the wrist chain to Jimmy, and he struggles to put it on his burned left wrist.

(grabbing it and putting it on Jimmy's other wrist) Look, the right side's just as good. Now let's get out of here and find us a pub.

JIMMY: *(he gathers up his box)* What about your hot nursie date?

GUS: Not to worry. I'll catch her up later and then give her the once over.

JIMMY: And one look at you and it'll be over.

GUS: Forget her, she's old news – if she can't say "Okotoks" without laughing, it's her loss. We've got some serious D.F.C. celebrating to do! Oh, uh, if you lend me a bob I'll stand you a pint, and we can get royally tanked up.

As they exit, Gus "back-boots" Jimmy in the seat of his pants. They exit.

SCENE 10

The sound of the cruising Halifax is heard. Slowly, the light of sunrise begins to come up. Jimmy and the crew are returning from their sortie, just a couple of miles off the English coast. Hillis is sitting at Skinner's feet and Gus is sitting half out of his navigator's position.

HILLIS: *(checking his elbows)* Oh, not again! If they're going to make me lie on my elbows down here, they could at least give me extra "elbow pay!"

FEVER: What's that big patch over there, Skip?

GUS: Where?

FEVER: There.

JIMMY: That's no spud-patch. That's the prettiest black and gray picture you'll ever want to see when your kite's in distress. Straight and long. Beats the coastline curves every time – just beautiful.

GUS: Skipper, if that's your only idea of good looking, we've just got to get you some female companionship!

FEVER: But what is it, Skip?

JIMMY: That is the big flat emergency welcome mat they call Woodbridge.

GUS: *(looking)* It sort of looks like they took all the roads in Canada and squeezed them together.

JIMMY: And I haven't had to use it once, have I?

SKINNER: No, Skip. I'll admit, you always bring us back with oh, at least a good whiff or two in the reserve tank!

> *Skinner quietly breaks wind. Everyone sniffs the bad smell and Gus starts wafting the air with his hands.*

GUS: Hell's bells! Give me a match!

JIMMY: It wasn't me!

GUS: Fever?

HILLIS: *(gasping)* Who let Göring on board?

GUS: Skinner!

SKINNER: *(defensive)* Hey, you're the guys who voted we should switch and have our eggs before Ops! I said, no, we should carry on like everyone else and have something to look forward to when we got back. But oh, no! You guys all of a sudden decide we should have them first...

GUS: ...because if we ever got the chop, they won't serve us eggs at the Luft Stalag Café! But you must be the only guy in the air force who can get fart-happy on powdered eggs!

HILLIS: Oh, Annie! Excuse me while I parachute out of the blue air!

Darby suddenly fires his guns as he sees an M.E.-109 bearing down on the Halifax.

DARBY: *(shouts on intercom)* Messerschmit! Messerschmit!

FRENCHY: *(shouts on intercom)* Fighter!

Everyone tries to scramble back to his position.

DARBY: *(still firing bursts)* Fighter! Fighter! Port quarter, level, 900 yards! M.E.-109!

A sudden burst of the ME's 20mm nose cannon tears through the perspex and into Jimmy, Skinner and Hillis. Jimmy is killed instantly, the 20mm rounds almost cutting him in two. Skinner is seriously wounded and Hillis is severely wounded but barely able to function.

GUS: *(shouting)* Jimmy! Jimmy! *(his intercom rips off from his head as he climbs up to Jimmy)*

DARBY: I got the son of a bitch! I got a piece of him! *(with his adrenaline pumping, he can't stop firing)*

HILLIS: *(shouting)* I'm hit! *(he shouts to Skinner)* Skinner?

Fever moves to tend to the wounded. Gus grabs the yoke in his left hand and Jimmy's head in his right. He frantically wipes the blood on his jacket.

FEVER: *(shouting)* We're going down!

Gus struggles to shove Jimmy out of the seat and then climbs past him and takes control of the Halifax. He pulls off Jimmy's headset and puts it on himself.

HILLIS: *(plugging in his intercom and shouting)* You? Can you land this thing for me, sir?

GUS: *(he concentrates on the controls)* You got any better ideas? Fever! Fever, I need you to radio Woodbridge! Fever!

FEVER: *(he pulls himself toward his wireless controls)* Yes, sir. I'm on my way...

GUS: I need you now, Fever!

FEVER: *(on the wireless)* Hello Woodbridge. Hello Woodbridge, this is Pickersgill "J" Jig, Pickersgill "J" Jig. Request priority, pilot and crew wounded on board; repeat, request priority, pilot and crew wounded. Over. *(relaying Woodbridge message)* Pickersgill "J" Jig. Identify with Avery colours. Identify with Avery colours immediately!

GUS: Darby, find the Avery Pistol and fire the Colours of the Day!

DARBY: Aye, Skipper. *(he finds the pistol and fires the flares down the chute)* Flares fired! Flares fired, Skip!

FEVER: Woodbridge, Woodbridge, this is Pickersgill "J" Jig; colours-of-the-day fired. Request priority, pilot and crew wounded on board; repeat, request priority, pilot and crew wounded. Over. *(relaying Woodbridge message)* Pickersgill "J" Jig, are you out of juice? Repeat, are you out of juice?

GUS: Darby, I'm going to need you to help me with the controls on approach. We'll only have one shot at it, so get Hillis to tell you what we need to do in what order.

DARBY: Aye, sir.

Darby crawls to Hillis and shouts at his ear, then Hillis shouts back.

GUS: *(he tries unsuccessfully to deploy the landing gear)* Darby! Fever! Start the hand crank on the landing gear!

DARBY: Aye, sir. *(he begins cranking down the landing gear)*

FEVER: Woodbridge, negative – juice okay, but navigator flying the aircraft. Repeat, navigator flying the aircraft. Over.

Fever joins Darby in cranking the landing gear.

GUS: Darby, turn on the landing lights to show we're a friendly.

Darby leaves the gear crank, turns on the landing lights and takes control of the flaps and throttles.

FEVER: *(relaying Woodbridge message)* Crash trucks on standby. We'll talk you down. Repeat, we'll talk you down.

The lights move the scene to the grounds of Woodbridge, with the wrecked Halifax on the ground. Fever, Darby and Frenchy remove Skinner, Hillis and the body of Jimmy. Gus remains seated in the cockpit, watching quietly. The light goes down on the a/c and follows Gus as he moves to take his seat in the Briefing Room. The black chalkboard and white chalk lines and writing of the Ops Board is projected on the faces of those in the Briefing Room. Several aircraft are marked as F.T.R.. Gus's hands shake. He cradles a hot mug of whiskey-laced coffee and lights a cigarette.

WOODBRIDGE BRIEFING OFFICER: So you lads are part of that new R.C.A.F. Group 6, is that right?

GUS: Yes, sir. Pickersgill.

WOODBRIDGE BRIEFING OFFICER: *(enters and sits)* Alright, well let's get just a few details and then you can get a good kip. How was the flak?

GUS: *(monotone)* Moderate stuff.

WOODBRIDGE BRIEFING OFFICER: Any night-fighters?

GUS: One.

WOODBRIDGE BRIEFING OFFICER: Oh, of course, yes. One is all it takes, isn't it. Did you see any of our kites go down?

GUS: Four.

WOODBRIDGE BRIEFING OFFICER: All bombs away?

GUS: Yes.

WOODBRIDGE BRIEFING OFFICER: No hang-ups?

GUS: *(looking up at the officer)* No.

WOODBRIDGE BRIEFING OFFICER: And did you get an aiming point photo?

GUS: Yes. I guess. I don't know.

WOODBRIDGE BRIEFING OFFICER: Well, you'll be pleased to know, overall it was a wizard prang. The preliminary reports suggest the target was well hit. I don't have the exact figures, but considering the size of the raid, the number of Failed to Return should be within expectations.

> *Gus stares at him.*

Further comments? No?

GUS: *(he takes Jimmy's wrist chain out of his pocket)* None.

WOODBRIDGE BRIEFING OFFICER: Very well, Minton. That was a good bit of work, bringing her in like that. Wish you hadn't destroyed the landing gear, but that couldn't be helped, I suppose. I expect you'll be getting a mention in dispatches for it, and quite probably a D.F.C. to boot. Tough about your mates, of course.

GUS: Yes, sir.

WOODBRIDGE BRIEFING OFFICER: Anything else?

GUS: No, sir.

WOODBRIDGE BRIEFING OFFICER: Very well. See the Orderly Officer. We've arranged a cot for you. I'll see that your Squadron is notified you're here, and we'll get you back there as soon as practical.

GUS: My crew...?

WOODBRIDGE BRIEFING OFFICER: I'll have someone check in on them once we get the hospital reports. That's all. *(he exits)*

The Ops Board fades out and Gus leaves the debriefing to fall into step behind a small R.C.A.F. Honour Guard. At Jimmy's grave the guards raise their rifles to fire three times, then march off. Gus remains at the graveside, holding Jimmy's wrist chain. The lights go down.

SCENE 11

A Harvard is heard passing low overhead. Betty, in her uniform overcoat and hauling a big duffle bag, arrives at Shirley's house.

SHIRLEY: *(off-stage)* Elizabeth! Is that you, dear?

BETTY: Hi, Mrs. Grady.

SHIRLEY: *(off-stage)* Have a seat. I'm putting my face on. I'll just be two shakes.

BETTY: No rush.

SHIRLEY: *(off-stage)* Have a look in Jimmy's parcel and see if there's anything I've forgotten.

Betty finds the box and half-heartedly looks through it.

(entering) Thanks for helping me take it to the post office. I think the more of them I send him, the bigger and heavier they get!

They hug one another.

It's good to see you again, dear. I think we should stop by the green grocer on the way and get some good apples, too. What do you think?

BETTY: This might already be over the weight limit, Mrs. G.

SHIRLEY: Oh, a couple of apples won't add much. And we can stop for a nice cup of tea and a biscuit afterward. *(she notices the large duffle bag)* What on earth? That looks just like James's...

BETTY: I'm going overseas.

SHIRLEY: What?

BETTY: I'm sorry but I won't be able to go to the post office. I've got to catch the train east at four.

SHIRLEY: Overseas? Where? For what?

BETTY: I'm staying on in the Royal Canadian Air Force Women's Division, but I'll be part of the R.A.F. A.T.A. – the Air Transport Auxiliary.

SHIRLEY: I never thought I'd see the day. It's not right, sending girls off to fight.

BETTY: I won't be in combat. I'll be flying planes back and forth between air bases and such. I'll probably never even set eyes on a German.

SHIRLEY: Still, I never thought I'd see it.

BETTY: Well, it never would have been possible if my Dad hadn't pulled a lot of strings.

SHIRLEY: What do you mean?

BETTY: All the pilots in the auxiliary are R.A.F. But my Dad was born in England and he still has a hand in the R.A.F., and I kept telling him how I wanted to fly. So he called in some favours. A few years back, the Auxiliary Commander's son was way up north in the bush here, and when his appendix suddenly burst, my Dad was the one who flew him to a hospital. Just in time, too. So, the old R.A.F. brass owed him. I guess I'll be the first and only Canadian woman in the A.T.A.

SHIRLEY: James always said you could fly circles around the boys.

BETTY: I just had more practice, I guess. At least this way, I'll get to fly all sorts of aeroplanes, if only for a few miles or so.

SHIRLEY: But most of the girls around here are thrilled to be working in the Women's Division. They've never had such opportunities outside the home.

BETTY: I know. "We serve so that men may fly." Women have come a long, long way in this war, but it's just not enough for me. I'm a flyer, Mrs. G., and the worst thing for a flyer is to be stuck on the ground.

SHIRLEY: Does James know?

BETTY: I told him in my last letter, but who knows when it actually gets there.

SHIRLEY: Do you know where you'll be stationed yet? Maybe you'll run into James?

BETTY: I wish I could, but I don't know, Mrs. G. England's a fairly big island.

SHIRLEY: Let me put a box together, for both of you, and you can take it with you and then look him up when you get there.

BETTY: I'd love to, but there's strict limits. All I'm allowed is my one duffle bag. If it doesn't fit in here, it doesn't go. Have you heard from Jimmy since you sent him the last big box full of goodies?

SHIRLEY: *(she pulls out a letter from her apron pocket, unfolds it and holds it up; it is mostly black bars)* He said "thanks" for I don't know what, and I think he likes his crew members – and of course he's palling around with Gus, but the censors blacked out what he seemed so excited about. Knowing Angus, that's probably just as well. I guess that boy still thinks of himself as a ladykiller.

BETTY: That's our Gus. One look at him and the girls just drop dead!

SHIRLEY: He always did look out for my boy, so I don't mind, I guess.

    Silence.

SHIRLEY: *(she pulls a sealed envelope from the box)* Well, if you can't take the box, can you at least take this to James, in case you do run into him? If you don't actually see him, you could put it in the military mail over there.

BETTY: Sure, although it'll probably be weeks before I'm actually crossing the Atlantic. It might do just as well if it's in the box.

SHIRLEY: No, I'd like you to take it. Oh, I'd feel a lot better if you just stayed on with your job here.

BETTY: *(she puts the envelope into her coat pocket)* I know.

SHIRLEY: Listen, I'm all alone out here, with Jimmy's Dad at the veterans hospital. You could come and stay here until Jimmy gets back. And you wouldn't have to pay for food or rent, so you could start saving up for your wedding. Or for the aeroplane service James always talks about.

BETTY: I'd like to, Mrs. Grady. And you're very kind. But I just have to get flying. It's in my blood, I guess. Besides, my transfer is already done, and you know how the air force hates to reverse any paper work.

SHIRLEY: My friend Grace's son joined up. The minute he turned eighteen, he went straight to the recruitment office. He didn't even have a bite of his birthday cake. She hasn't heard one word from him since he went overseas. Please tell me you and James won't get married over there. Wait until you both come home, and we can do it up big here.

BETTY: I might not get posted anywhere near Jimmy.

SHIRLEY: I know, but if you do get together, wait, please.

BETTY: I'll try. That's all I can do. Anyway, I'll probably be so busy flying all the time, I won't have any time to fraternize at all. But I'll try.

As Betty leans in to a hug, Shirley halfheartedly returns it.

SHIRLEY: *(as she puts the censored letter back in her apron pocket, she pulls out a newspaper clipping and looks at it)* Why did they change it?

BETTY: Change what?

SHIRLEY: The notices in the paper. Since the war started it's been "Died In Service". And now all of a sudden it's "Casualty List (Air Force)." No notice, no explanation. Why would they do that?

BETTY: I didn't know it was different.

SHIRLEY: Different? It's not right. Boys are dying in service – they're not *(almost spitting it out)* "casualties."

132

BETTY: I guess, because there's more things happening, like aircrew getting captured, reported missing…

SHIRLEY: Well it's a slap in the face to people whose boys are killed. Our neighbour, the Rawlins, across the road on the next section, their boy "Died In Service." He wasn't just a polite "Casualty." Why can't the damned air force have any respect?

Betty hugs Shirley, and this time the older woman reciprocates.

I'm sorry, dear.

BETTY: It's okay, Mrs. Grady.

SHIRLEY: The longer this war goes on, the more I find myself doing things a mother shouldn't – at least, things a patriotic mother shouldn't. May I go with you down to the train station? I won't make a fuss, I promise.

BETTY: Of course. And you'd better make a fuss.

SHIRLEY: You'll be boarding a train full of crazy young men. You'll be fussed over from here to Nova Scotia. *(serious)* Just please be careful. We're all in the same war, but England's a heck of a lot closer to it than the Canadian prairies.

BETTY: I promise. I'll be careful. Now, we'd better hurry, or I'll get reprimanded before I even report to the R.A.F.

Betty slings her duffle bag over her shoulder, picks up the box, and the two women leave together.

SCENE 12

Gus is sitting on his haunches outside his barracks. Graziano, now a Squadron Leader pilot, enters, unseen by Gus. He carries a duffle bag and stops when he sees Gus.

GRAZIANO: *(he alters his voice)* Hello. I guess I'm your new pilot. R.C.A.F. Flight Lieutenant Grant March, No.4 Flying School, Saskatoon.

GUS: *(still not looking at Graziano)* No disrespect, sir, but please don't tell me who you are. I don't want to know it.

GRAZIANO: Doesn't sound so friendly coming from a fellow Canuck.

GUS: *(still not looking up)* If I don't know your name, I won't have it to forget.

GRAZIANO: Well, now, that works both ways, doesn't it. Nobody's going to know you. Besides, you might just be pleasantly surprised.

GUS: *(standing and extending his hand, head still down)* Flying Officer Angus Minton., No.2 Observer School, Edmonton... *(he finally looks Graziano in the eye)* Gratz? Graziano? What the hell?

GRAZIANO: In the flesh! It's good to see you, Gus.

Gus embraces Graziano.

GUS: Jeeze! I can't believe it! But your family – and I thought the air force wouldn't take you?

GRAZIANO: The R.C.A.F. wouldn't take Graziano Marchitelli – but they had open arms for Grant March and his civilian pilot's license.

GUS: So you diddled your name.

GRAZIANO: Papa's idea. He said, "Do like the Jews and change your name. So long as you know who you are inside, it doesn't matter what you call yourself." And that's how Grant March came to be welcomed with wide-open arms into the R.C.A.F. That and the rising losses.

GUS: But after all they put your family through, you still wanted to join up?

GRAZIANO: Well, they did take my Papa away, but I scrounged around the house and finally found his Canadian citizenship papers. Then I went to that damn internment camp out in the Kananaskis every week to see him, and every week I politely waved those papers under the nose of the Mountie in charge. And then they decided they were going to transfer him to a camp in Petawawa way out in Ontario, so I had to think fast. Good ol' Mama had the answer: bribery by sausage! Italian sweet sausage to be exact!

GUS: I don't get it.

GRAZIANO: Meat has been rationed in Canada, so Mama said to take the Mountie a couple of her mouth-watering sweet sausages, and just like that *(he snaps his fingers),* the corporal suddenly determined that his papers were good enough, and he kicked Papa out. And my uncles came down from Edmonton to help, so they made sure regular deliveries of the bribe were made afterward, until the corporal got transferred to some other camp or somewhere. My Papa got to come home, and one day he just told me if I still wanted to fly and join up, I had his blessing. So, with the slight identity adjustment and a couple of doctored papers, off I went, joined up, and here I am. When the war's over I'm going to get my law degree so I can sue the pants off the R.C.M.P. or Canada or somebody for what they put my family through.

GUS: I can't believe it! It's so great to see you again! *(quiet)* Jimmy's gone.

GRAZIANO: I know.

GUS: *(he holds up a 20mm round)* It was an M.E.109. Cut him in half with the nose-cannon. Right in half. This one was lodged in the bone of his spine.

GRAZIANO: Jesus.

GUS: It's not good, Gratz. Every night, whole sections are getting torn to shreds. The biggest column on every station's Ops board is Failed To Return. That's why I don't want to know anybody's name any more. New guys come in one night and by the next morning they're F.T.R. and never seen again. Some guys don't even unpack their shaving kit, for god's sake – then it's one sortie and they're gone. Just gone. Lost.

GRAZIANO: I know. Back home, they're pushing guys through with less and less ground school and air training, just to keep up. You guys went through with sixty to seventy hours just in Elementary, but the hours are nowhere near that many, now. *(forced levity)* Hell, they even sent me. *(serious)* I know it's bad, Gus. But overall, the whole war, it's starting to turn – slow as glaciers maybe, but it is turning.

GUS: He didn't do it right.

GRAZIANO: What?

GUS: *(angry)* When we filled in the gravestone form, the inscription was based on the number of letters and digits. So we figured out the best time to die was May in the first nine days, and that would leave more room for sappy verse inscriptions. He should have died on the right day in the right month – he didn't do it right. It was just something we did. You wouldn't understand.

GRAZIANO: Listen. It's okay. It's okay, Gus. *(he grabs one of Gus's shoulders)* It's okay. He's flying up there now, buzzing Saint Peter – flying all around, what did he call it? "Wings" or something?

GUS: *(quietly)* Something like that.

GRAZIANO: Anyway, he's doing exactly what he loved. *(pause)* You know how you can always tell a pilot in heaven?

GUS: 'Cause he's the only one dying to get back to flying. *(trailing off)* You can always tell a pilot...

GRAZIANO: But you can't tell him much.

GUS: His mother's never even going to see his grave.

GRAZIANO: I know, but once the war is over, you and Betty could fly her over.

GUS: She's the best Mom I ever knew – she loved him to bits. She's going to get one of those regret letters, but they never say the horrible details, the terrible way he got it – all the horrible details about how our boys are getting killed. Some are just knocked to spots up there, but their families never know.

GRAZIANO: It has to be that way, you know that. It's best they never know, especially for Mrs. Grady.

GUS: But why him? Why not me? Why couldn't that stupid Kraut have aimed two feet forwards, so's it'd be him standing here, not me?

GRAZIANO: *(quietly)* I don't know. You can knock on Saint Peter's door, but it's still up to him whether he thinks it's your time or not. *(pause)* Listen. The brass has a new squadron in the works. It'll be made up of the very best pilots and navigators. I'm one of them, and I want you to be my Nav.

GUS: For what?

GRAZIANO: *(he looks about him to ensure that he's not overheard)* It's still all very hush-hush, so you can't tell a soul. They're going to have this new squadron fly the lead-in on all the raids. They'll go in to the exact location, and then mark the target area with colour-coded incendiaries so's the bombers coming behind will know exactly where to hit. They're tagging them as Pathfinders, and only the best of the best will get the job. Interested?

Gus breathes deeply and exhales.

I hear you're up for a gong after your landing heroics – probably a D.F.C. We can start as soon as the official jazz is over and done with. Oh, and this new squadron has a new bird, too – an Avro Lancaster with four big Rolls Royce Merlins; they're inline, so they purr right along, or so I'm told. Come on, Angus. What do you want, do you want me to beg?

Graziano begins to kneel.

GUS: Alright, alright. Get up, before somebody sees. What the hell – I'll do it.

GRAZANO: That's the ticket. Come on, I've got to find my bunk, and then we can find us a pub.

Gus grabs the duffle bag, and he and Graziano exit together.

SCENE 13

The general lighting begins to fade, as the light on Shirley's farmhouse gradually comes up to dim.

COMMANDER VOICE: Dear Mr. Grady. I deeply regret to inform you that your son, #R.U. 27433, Pilot Officer James Edgerton Grady, gave his life in the service of his country on sixteen-seventeen August, nineteen-hundred and forty-three, in the European Theatre of war. Your son was an excellent pilot and a fine leader. He and his crew performed admirably in whatever task they were assigned. James' boys were nearing the end of their first tour when they were attacked by a German night-fighter in the skies over the English Channel. You may take solace in the fact that your son was likely killed instantly and therefore would not have suffered. A package containing your son's personal effects will follow under separate cover.

A Calgary Herald newspaper thuds onto the porch. A second hits, and then a third. The light slowly fades to black.

138

EPILOGUE

As a downstage light comes up, Betty, in her R.C.A.F. W.D.
uniform and overcoat and carrying her duffle bag, enters and
marches into the lit area.

BETTY: R.C.A.F. airmen will serve overseas in various commands on
operations in various theatres of war around the world. But most will
fly for Bomber Command, out of bases in England and Scotland,
flying mostly Halifax and then Lancaster bombers.

In 1943, No.6 Group was formed, made entirely of thirteen Canadian
squadrons serving under Bomber Command. They will fly over forty
thousand sorties, drop over one hundred and twenty-six thousand
bombs, and lose more than eight hundred aircraft. And those Canadian
aircrews will collect some eight thousand medals – eight thousand of
the most tangible of all recognitions of valour, courage, duty, worn
upon the left breast, over the heart.

In Bomber Command over the nearly six years of the war, the
Canadians with the Royal Air Force, and all of the other
Commonwealth aircrews will fly over three hundred and ninety-two
thousand sorties. They will drop some nine hundred and fifty-five
thousand bombs, and more than ten thousand aircraft will be lost.

(she pauses) Lost just doesn't cut it – lost is what your family dog gets
sometimes. Lost is the love of a sweetheart sometimes. But most
times, those will be followed by the wonderful relief and joy of being
newly found again.

When aircraft are lost, they don't ever come back. They are never
again found. Lost is an airborne coffin containing as many as seven
aircrew – seven young men, boys, most of them, all perishing amid the
flames and destruction and utter disintegration of machine and men,
boys. Nearly fifty-five thousand airmen, lost – nearly sixty percent of
all who flew. Ten thousand of those will be Canadian men, boys, lost.
As much as thirty thousand feet above the earth, plummeting,
exploding, lost to the wind; men, boys, never to become found – lost.

No, Bomber Command will be no piece of cake.

During the following, the lights come up behind her to silhouette seven airmen at attention spaced evenly across the stage.

Of every one hundred aircrew flying under that command, fifty-one will be killed on Ops. *(the first airman drops his head and exits)*

Nine will die in crashes in England. *(the second airman drops his head and exits)*

Three will be seriously injured. *(the third airman grabs his shoulder with his opposite hand, collapses his torso slightly and exits)*

Twelve will be captured and become guests of Stalag Luftwaffe as Prisoners of War. *(the fourth airman clasps his hands behind his head and exits)*

One will actually evade capture. *(the fifth airman cautiously exits)*

And barely twenty-four will survive unharmed. *(the sixth and seventh airmen remain at attention)* Twenty-four of one hundred. Less than twenty-five percent of aircrew will survive their tour of thirty sorties.

The casualties and the time lags and the lists – printed in the R.C.A.F.'s *Wings Abroad* newspapers and newspapers throughout Canada – so very many lists to keep track of:

Killed in Action.

Previously Reported Missing, Believed Killed in Action, Now Presumed Killed in Action.

Previously Reported Missing, Now Presumed Killed in Action.

Missing, Believed Killed in Action.

Died of Wounds or Injuries Received in Action.

Missing.

Killed On Active Service.

Previously Reported Missing, Now Reported Prisoner of War.

Previously Reported Missing, Believed Killed on Active Service, Now Presumed Killed on Active Service

Died on Active Service.

Previously Reported Missing, Now Presumed Killed on Active Service.

And still, the volunteers, they keep coming, keep pouring into the ranks of the R.C.A.F. Mr. Churchill will soon tell the world that it owes its eventual freedom to the men, the boys, of Bomber Command, calling their service: "a duty nobly done."

Canada will remain at war to the very end: six long, hard, heart-breaking years. The men, and women, who served in the Royal Canadian Air Force will distinguish themselves in the name of Canada and all the free world. And for their outstanding bravery under fire, six Canadian airmen will be awarded the Victoria Cross, the Commonwealth's greatest military honour.

And we will remember them.

For those who served, those who flew,
those who touched shed angels' wings.

They will be remembered.

> *Overlapping voice-overs of several "regrets letters" from a selection of Commanding Officers echo and replay around the theatre. During these voice-overs, Betty slowly turns and exits.*

COMMANDER VOICES: "Dear Mr. Breverton: I regret to inform you..."

"Dear Mr. Hillis: I regret to inform you that your son, #R.W. 22489, Flight Sergeant Harold K. Hillis, gave his life in the service of his country..."

"Dear Mr. Brébuf: I regret to inform you..."

"Dear Mr. Williams..."

"Dear Mr. Felverton: I regret to inform you that your son, #S.V. 32663, Flight Sergeant Francis Felverton..."

"Dear Mr..."

"Dear Mr. Bradfield..."

"...R.A.F. Flight Engineer Fred Langdon gave his life..."

"Dear Mr. Gibson: I regret..."

"...Mr. Sanders... Flight Lieutenant Algernon Sanders gave his life..."

"...Gunner, Wilber Hornby..."

"...Air Gunner Quintin Darby... in the service of his country..."

"...Mr. Peterson: I regret to inform you..."

"...Bomb Aimer Andrew Patrick Mills lost his life..."

"...your son... Pilot Charles Middlesbe gave his life..."

"...I regret to inform you..."

"...Taylor gave his life in the service of his country..."

"...Mr. Harris: I regret..."

"...Pilot Officer Gary Michael Ward, gave his life..."

"...Breverton lost his life..."

"...Kirkpatrick, gave his life..."

"...regret to..."

"...Thornton: I regret to inform you..."

"...Mr. Green: I regret..."

"...your son, #R.S. 53433, Navigator, Robert Thomas Root..."

"...Andrew Gillian..."

"...Smith, lost his life..."

"...lost his life..."

"...gave his life..."

"...lost his life..."

"...gave his life..."

"...lost his life..."

"...gave his life..."

As the voices fade out, a tune such as the "Air Force March" strikes up, the Recruiting Officer returns to his station down right and begins signing up a young civilian.

Four A.C.2s in sweatpants and sweatshirts enter, form a line facing downstage, bend over and lower their pants to reveal their upper buttocks. The Corporal enters, throws up his arms in disgust. The A.C.2s pull up their pants, then turn upstage and all repeat in mime the "short arm inspection" of ACT 1, SCENE 2.

As the music continues, Tiger Moths and Harvards are heard flying overhead.

Blackout.

THE END

APPENDIX I   EXPLANATION OF TERMS

Beam: a directional radio wave Morse Code signal used to fix a navigational position.

Colours of the Day: a selected designation of colour flares to be fired in the case of emergency. By flaring the correct colour on a given day, the air base would know the incoming a/c is not enemy.

Corkscrewing: an evasive manoeuvre whereby the pilot sends the a/c into a diving and twisting action.

East Grinstead Queen Victoria Hospital: a British hospital in the town of the same name, renowned for its pioneering work in treating burns of airmen. A wing of the hospital was dedicated to the Canadians where Canadian Dr. Ross Tilley pioneered the treatment and recuperation of badly burned airmen.

Erk: slang for ground crew aircraftsmen.

Fat can word play in Act One Scene 14: Shirley's use of the term refers to a can for collecting cooking fat. Hillis's use refers to adipose deposits on the buttocks.

Feathering or windmilling: setting the propeller of a damaged or useless engine to zero drag configuration. *Port inner* refers to the engine closest to the fuselage, on the left or pilot's side.

Flare: the process of increasing the lift and the angle of attack of the a/c's wing, to arrest the sink rate of the a/c, just above the runway, prior to actual touchdown.

Gosport: a crude, funnel-shaped, *Bakelite* apparatus sticking out of the instrument panel. Used to facilitate communication between instructor and student.

Happy Valley: R.A.F./R.C.A.F. slang for the Ruhr Valley.

NAAFI: the acronym for the U.K.s Navy, Army and Air Force Institutes that provided support and leisure services to enlisted men and women.

Perspex: the clear plastic glass used in a/c windows.

Snap-roll: an aerobatic manoeuvre whereby the a/c is rolled through inverted while maintaining altitude.

Sprog: a new flying recruit.

Strike hard! Strike sure!: The battle cry on the crest of Bomber Command.

Woodbridge: an especially wide long air strip near the east coast of England, designed for use by severely damaged or distressed Allied a/c.

APPENDIX II   SETTING FOR EACH SCENE

ACT ONE

Scene 1	No.3 Recruiting Depot (R.D.), Calgary, Alberta
Scene 2	No.3 Manning Depot (M.D.), Edmonton, Alberta
Scene 3, 4	No.4 Initial Training School (I.T.S.), Edmonton, Alberta
Scenes 5-11	No.5 Elementary Flying Training School (E.F.T.S.), High River, Alberta
Scenes 12, 13	No.3 Service Flying Training School (S.F.T.S.), Calgary, Alberta
Scene 14	City of Calgary, Alberta
Scenes 15, 16	No.3 Service Flying Training School (S.F.T.S.), Calgary, Alberta

ACT TWO

Scene 1	No.3 Pilot Reception Centre, Bournemouth, England
Scenes 2-4	Pickersgill Air Base, England (fictional town and air base, R.A.F. Bomber Command)
Scene 5	City of Calgary, Alberta
Scene 6	Halifax Aircraft, over Occupied Europe
Scene 7	Shirley's farmhouse near No.3 S.F.T.S., Calgary, Alberta
Scene 8	Pickersgill Air Base, England (Bomber Command)
Scene 9	East Grinstead Queen Victoria Airmen's Hospital
Scene 10	Halifax Aircraft, approaching the east coast of England and Woodbridge Air Base
Scene 11	Shirley's farmhouse near No.3 S.F.T.S., Calgary, Alberta
Scene 12	Pickersgill Air Base, England (Bomber Command)

APPENDIX III   CHARACTERS IN ORDER OF APPEARANCE

ACT ONE

PROLOGUE   Betty

1   Recruitment Sergeant, Older man, Jimmy, Gus, Graziano, Betty
2   Gus, Jimmy, Recruits, Corporal, Pilot White, Pilot Black
3   Jimmy, Gus, Chipper, A/C Recognition Instructor Voice, Health
     Instructor, Recruits
4   Jimmy, Gus, Psychology Officer
5   Chipper, LACs, Jimmy, Civilian Flight Instructor Chalmers
6   Gus, Civilian Flight Instructor Reid
7   Commanding Officer, Shirley, Jimmy
8   Gus, Jimmy
9   Jimmy, Civilian Flight Instructor Chalmers
10   Chief Flying Instructor, Gus, Jimmy, LACs
11   Corporal, Jimmy, LACs
12   Jimmy, R.C.A.F. Instructor, Shirley
13   Chipper, Jimmy, LACs
14   Shirley, Hillis
15   Jimmy
16   LACs, Corporal Voice, Group Captain, Shirley, Betty, Jimmy,
     Gus
17   Gus, Jimmy, New Recruits, Corporal

ACT TWO

1   Drill Sergeant Voice, Jimmy, Gus, Hillis, Darby, Frenchy,
     Veteran Flight Engineer
2   Jimmy, Gus
3   Jimmy, Gus, Hillis, Darby, Frenchy, Fever, Skinner,
     Commanding Officer Voice, Meteorology Officer Voice
4   Jimmy, Gus, Hillis, Darby, Frenchy, Fever, Skinner
5   Policeman/Saboteur, Shirley, Grace
6   Jimmy, Gus, Hillis, Darby, Frenchy, Fever, Skinner
7   Shirley
8   Gus, Darby
9   Jimmy, Hannigan, Gus
10   Jimmy, Gus, Hillis, Darby, Frenchy, Fever, Skinner, Woodbridge
     Briefing Officer
11   Betty, Shirley
12   Gus, Graziano
13   Commander Voice

EPILOGUE   Betty, Commander Voices

APPENDIX IV   NOTES TO DIRECTORS AND PRODUCER

UNIFORMS: Standard issue, ill-fitting R.C.A.F. uniforms are made of wool. Upon receipt, recruits would have to take them to a local tailor to have the sleeves, cuffs, etc. fitted properly. When the airmen are posted on Ops, they are issued a short battle-dress uniform jacket, to be used when flying. Officers wear their light blue bars on sleeve cuffs. At all times, all members of the R.C.A.F. are to be impeccable.

GENERAL BEHAVIOUR: Personnel march in tight formation with the distinct R.C.A.F. shoulder-high swing of their arms, and they snap to attention for any other order. Very rarely are a man's hands to be seen in his pants pockets while in uniform, and rarely if ever in the pockets of his jacket/tunic. The snap to attention has the right knee up to waist high and then down.

Literally all elements and props from the 1940s are heavy. Ammunition boxes are very heavy. Flying suits and boots are fully lined to protect against unheated and unpressurized a/c, and, consequently, are very hot and uncomfortable when the wearer is not aboard an a/c. Cigarettes are unfiltered and smokers routinely pick bits of tobacco from their tongues or spit it out.

GENERAL NATURE OF SETTINGS: E.F.T.S. bases were civilian air bases, subcontracted to train R.C.A.F. students. All but the most senior personnel were civilian, including the flight instructors and ground school instructors, all overseen by an R.C.A.F. Commanding Officer. The food, accommodations, and other services were civilian-run, and the overall feel of the base was more casual and relaxed than a strict air force base. Although they were in proper uniform, the students were more civilian flying students than R.C.A.F. recruits at that point.

S.F.T.S. bases were fully operated by the R.C.A.F. with all the R.C.A.F. discipline and regimen that entails.

Aircrew recruits were never posted to training schools in their home province, but for the purposes of this play, Alberta recruits are trained in Alberta.

Producers are encouraged to represent the distinctive scents and odours associated with R.C.A.F. flights during the war, particularly the smells of wool, aviation oil, heavy canvas fabric and ammunition cordite.

MUSIC: Possibilities include titles from the early 1940s such as the traditional Canadian *Air Force March* and *The Maple Leaf Forever,* and big band swing music such as *I'll Never smile Again, Don't Sit Under the Apple Tree, Shake Down the Stars, I'll Be Seeing You, Blue Skies, I'm Getting Sentimental Over You, P.S. I Love You* and *Moonlight Serenade.*

REPRESENTATION OF AIRCRAFT: Possibilities include actors in full-scale replicas on stage, or actors simply using props and mime inside a cockpit made from lighting. Unless otherwise indicated, engine noise should first be established, and then the volume adjusted down or up, to facilitate dialogue and dramatic effect.

The De Haviland Tiger Moth is an elementary, light, radial engine biplane, requiring the sounds of a similar a/c. The North American Harvard is an advanced, heavy, low-winged monoplane with a very distinctive screaming nine-cylinder radial engine. The correct audio can be found in the film "Captains of the Clouds". The Handley-Page Halifax has four Hercules radial engines. Except for the Halifax, many of these old faithful war birds are still in existence and many are still flying, so it would be ideal to use actual recordings of all a/c, especially the particular screaming engine of the Harvard. Sound recordings of such a/c, including restored WWII a/c at modern air shows, can be purchased from many air museums. A recording of one of the only two existing flying Avro Lancasters, sister bomber to the Halifax, would be an appropriate substitute for the sound of a Halifax. Sounds of an M.E.109 and its machine guns are available on BBC sound effects recordings. Only the nose cannon fire of the second attacking M.E. 109 is audible to the Halifax crew.

Aeroplane controls vary: the Tiger Moth has a plain stick, the Harvard, a "spade-handle" stick, while the Halifax has a control yoke, a stick surmounted by a half-circle wheel with aileron and elevator surface controls attached.

APPENDIX V   SCHOOL PRODUCTION NOTES

If your school is unable to produce the entire play, consider performing a selection of scenes, especially for events such as Remembrance Day ceremonies.

Contact your closest Royal Canadian Legion (or equivalent) and nearest museum for research and information on WWII and the Royal Canadian Air Force. Contact your local historical archives or newspaper archives to research the era and determine if there was a British Commonwealth Air Training Plan air base near you and research it for your production. If a nearby base still exists, use photographs of it for scene background and publicity.

Visit and research the graves of R.C.A.F. airmen in your local cemeteries and monuments. Obtain biographical material on local service personnel through interviews and newspaper files. Prepare representations of graves for publicity.

Contact your local Canadian Air Cadets (or equivalent) for assistance with conducting precision marching in scenes in their Cadet uniforms (such as the *Wings Parade* scene), or as non-speaking acting roles (such as Erks or other Recruits or Bomber Crews).

Incorporate your production into your school's history classes, and if your school has a music program with an active band, have the band dress as either 1940's civilians or R.C.A.F. band members and play big band music for the play. If your school has an art program, student artists might work on the scenery and props, draw or paint characters, scenes, or aircraft, and help with publicity displays.

Invite veterans and/or the relatives of veterans to attend the play as guests of the school. Consider photographing veterans with the cast and presenting copies of the play and photos to the veterans.

If your community has a seniors care facility, speak to the recreation coordinator about a group visit to the play. Consider a publicity presentation at the facility to develop interest in attendance.

ACKNOWLEDGEMENTS

Scenes from the play have been published in the USA by Brooklyn Publishers (2000 - 2005). Scenes have appeared in the play anthologies Even More Monologues for Women by Women, Heinemann Drama (2001) and in Audition Monologues for Young Actors, Meriwether Publishers, (2001). Hannigan's monologue in Act Two won the Aero Space Museum Association of Calgary Silver Jubilee National Writing Competition, 2000, and was published in Fly Past Magazine, (2002). The playwright is proud to report that she has flown aerobatics and taken the stick several times in Canadian WWII aircraft, including a North American Harvard Mk IV (#20474, Arcot Aviation) and in a Boeing Stearman (#CF-QJV, Sunwest Aviation).

The playwright wishes to express her gratitude for the support of her family, especially to her brother Art, who shares with her his love of flying and to Sharyn, who believes in what her playwright sister does. The playwright also gratefully acknowledges the Alberta Foundation for the Arts, the Alberta Historical Resources Foundation, Sherring Amsden, Finnegan Armour, Gael Blackhall, Brian Brennan, Carole Clement, Sandra De Helen, Cecelia and John Frey, Maggi and Stewart Hunter, the International Centre for Women Playwrights ListServ, Michael McCabe, John Murrell, John Neal, Gary Radjo, and the Halifax 57 Rescue Canada restoration project.

The aircraft image on the cover is taken, with permission, from Michael McCabe's painting "Invincible Item". It depicts the Handley Page Halifax B Mk.III, LW170 of R.C.A.F. 424 Squadron homeward bound in August of 1944 after her twenty-sixth combat operation.

The original painting was donated to Halifax 57 Rescue (Canada) by the artist in memory of his cousin, Halifax tail gunner William D. Walsh. Halifax 57 Rescue (Canada) is proceeding in 2006 with plans to recover LW170 from its underwater resting place. Funding of this project will be assisted by sales of limited-edition prints of "Invincible Item", signed by the artist and extant crew members.

Information regarding print purchases: Halifax 57 Rescue (Canada). Address: Suite 212 – 2980 Colonial Road, Sarsfield, ON, K0A 3E0 Web address: http://www.57rescuecanada.com Phone: 613 835 1748

ABOUT THE AUTHOR

Sandra Dempsey is an award winning Calgary playwright whose work has been produced in North America and Europe. Her plays are noted for their vivid characterizations and vibrant dialogues, as well as for their acerbic wit and unique, sensitive styling. Her writing is uncompromising, compassionate and impassioned. It powerfully reflects her own view of her art: "To have the power in one's fingertips, one's words… is to have hands that can bridge the widest divide, and that is powerful beyond all the black powder in the world."